Junior Great Books

5

BOOK ONE

Junior Great Books®

5

Honesty
Self-Respect
Fitting In

BOOK ONE

**Great
Books**
Foundation

Copyright © 2014 by The Great Books Foundation

Chicago, Illinois

All rights reserved

ISBN 978-1-939014-52-8

4   6   8   9   7   5   3

Printed in the United States of America

Published and distributed by

THE GREAT BOOKS FOUNDATION

A nonprofit educational organization

233 North Michigan Avenue, Suite 420

Chicago, IL 60601

www.greatbooks.org

CONTENTS

INTRODUCTION

Welcome to Junior Great Books! In this program, you will be reading stories and discussing your ideas about them. Before you begin, here are some important things to know.

The stories in Junior Great Books will make you wonder about things. You might wonder what a word means, why the author told the story this way, or why a character does something. That's because authors do not usually tell us exactly how the parts of a story are connected or explain why everything in a story happens.

But in good writing, everything fits together and is there for a reason, even if it is not completely explained for you. Good authors put into their writing the things a reader must know to understand what is happening and why. As a good reader, you need to look closely at the writing to discover these things. In Junior Great Books, you will use a learning process called **Shared Inquiry**™ to help you do that.

How Shared Inquiry Works

In Shared Inquiry, you read stories that make you think and ask questions.

Usually you will begin work on a story by reading along as you hear the story read aloud. After everyone has read the story, the group shares questions about it. Any question you have about the story is worth asking. Some questions can be answered right away. Others will be saved for the discussion or other activities.

Next, everyone reads the story again. During the second reading you will do some activities that will help you understand the story better. These activities may include taking notes, sharing your thoughts about the story with a partner, or acting out scenes from the story.

You will then develop your ideas about the story even more in **Shared Inquiry discussion.**

In your discussion, you will sit so that everyone can see and hear one another. Your teacher will start the discussion with an **interpretive question**—a question that has more than one good answer that can be supported with evidence from the story. So in Shared Inquiry discussion, the teacher isn't looking for the "right answer" to the question, but is interested in hearing different ideas about it.

During the discussion, the teacher asks more questions that help everyone think deeply and explain their ideas.

Besides sharing your ideas, you can agree or disagree with a classmate or ask someone a question about a comment. You can also ask someone to explain an idea.

At the end of the discussion, people will have different answers to the interpretive question. But everyone will have evidence for his or her answer and a better understanding of the story. You may change your answer because of what you hear in the discussion, or you may hear new evidence to support your original answer.

After the discussion, you may do other activities based on the story. You may write about your answer to the discussion question or do a creative writing activity. Or you may make artwork, compose a song, or do research about something in the story.

You may find that even after the class has finished working on a story, you are still thinking about it. The characters and events in a story may help you think about your own life and the people around you in new ways, or suggest a new subject you are interested in.

Every time you ask a question about a story or discuss an interpretive question with your classmates, you are increasing your skills as a reader and thinker. You are also learning how stories work and what kinds of stories you enjoy. You are becoming a better reader.

DO

Let other people talk, and listen to what they say.

DON'T

Talk while other people are talking.

DO

Share your ideas about the story. You may have an idea no one else has thought of.

DON'T

Be afraid to say what you're thinking about the story.

DO
Be polite when
you disagree with
someone.

DON'T
Get angry when
someone disagrees
with you.

DO
Pay attention
to the person who
is talking.

DON'T
Do things that make
it hard for people
to pay attention.

Shared Inquiry Discussion Guidelines

Following these guidelines in Shared Inquiry discussion will help everyone share ideas about the story and learn from one another.

1 Listen to or read the story twice before the discussion.

2 Discuss only the story that everyone has read.

3 Support your ideas with evidence from the story.

4 Listen to other people's ideas. You may agree or disagree with someone's answer, or ask a question about it.

5 Expect the teacher to only ask questions.

Theme Introduction

Honesty

In this section of the book, you will read about characters who act honestly and characters who act dishonestly. Thinking about these stories, and about your own experiences being honest and dishonest, will give you new ideas about what it means to be honest.

Important Questions to Think About

Before starting this section, think about your own experiences with honesty:

- Can you think of a time when you or someone else didn't tell the truth?

- How do you feel when you realize someone has not been honest with you?

Once you have thought about your own experiences with honesty, think about this **theme question** and write down your answers or share them aloud:

Why might someone choose to behave honestly or dishonestly?

After reading each story in this section, ask yourself the theme question again. You may have some new ideas you want to add.

"Charles didn't even do exercises."

CHARLES

Shirley Jackson

The day my son Laurie started kindergarten he renounced corduroy overalls with bibs and began wearing blue jeans with a belt; I watched him go off the first morning with the older girl next door, seeing clearly that an era of my life was ended, my sweet-voiced nursery-school tot replaced by a long-trousered, swaggering character who forgot to stop at the corner and wave goodbye to me.

He came home the same way, the front door slamming open, his cap on the floor, and the voice suddenly become raucous shouting, "Isn't anybody *here*?"

At lunch he spoke insolently to his father, spilled his baby sister's milk, and remarked that his teacher said we were not to take the name of the Lord in vain.

"How *was* school today?" I asked, elaborately casual.

"All right," he said.

"Did you learn anything?" his father asked.

Laurie regarded his father coldly. "I didn't learn nothing," he said.

"Anything," I said. "Didn't learn anything."

"The teacher spanked a boy, though," Laurie said, addressing his bread and butter. "For being fresh," he added, with his mouth full.

"What did he do?" I asked. "Who was it?"

Laurie thought. "It was Charles," he said. "He was fresh. The teacher spanked him and made him stand in a corner. He was awfully fresh."

"What did he do?" I asked again, but Laurie slid off his chair, took a cookie, and left, while his father was still saying, "See here, young man."

The next day Laurie remarked at lunch, as soon as he sat down, "Well, Charles was bad again today." He grinned enormously and said, "Today Charles hit the teacher."

"Good heavens," I said, mindful of the Lord's name, "I suppose he got spanked again?"

14

"He sure did," Laurie said. "Look up," he said to his father.

"What?" his father said, looking up.

"Look down," Laurie said. "Look at my thumb. Gee, you're dumb." He began to laugh insanely.

"Why did Charles hit the teacher?" I asked quickly.

"Because she tried to make him color with red crayons," Laurie said. "Charles wanted to color with green crayons so he hit the teacher and she spanked him and said nobody play with Charles but everybody did."

The third day—it was Wednesday of the first week—Charles bounced a see-saw onto the head of a little girl and made her bleed, and the teacher made him stay inside all during recess. Thursday Charles had to stand in a corner during story time because he kept pounding his feet on the floor. Friday Charles was deprived of blackboard privileges because he threw chalk.

On Saturday I remarked to my husband, "Do you think kindergarten is too unsettling for Laurie? All this toughness, and bad grammar, and this Charles boy sounds like such a bad influence."

"It'll be all right," my husband said reassuringly. "Bound to be people like Charles in the world. Might as well meet them now as later."

On Monday Laurie came home late, full of news. "Charles," he shouted as he came up the hill; I was waiting anxiously on the front steps. "Charles," Laurie yelled all the way up the hill, "Charles was bad again."

"Come right in," I said, as soon as he came close enough. "Lunch is waiting."

"You know what Charles did?" he demanded, following me through the door. "Charles yelled so in school they sent a boy in from first grade to tell the teacher she had to make Charles keep quiet, and so Charles had to stay after school. And so all the children stayed to watch him."

"What did he do?" I asked.

"He just sat there," Laurie said, climbing into his chair at the table. "Hi, Pop, y'old dust mop."

"Charles had to stay after school today," I told my husband. "Everyone stayed with him."

"What does this Charles look like?" my husband asked Laurie. "What's his other name?"

"He's bigger than me," Laurie said. "And he doesn't have any rubbers and he doesn't ever wear a jacket."

Monday night was the first Parent-Teachers meeting, and only the fact that the baby had a cold kept me from going; I wanted passionately to meet Charles's mother. On Tuesday Laurie remarked suddenly, "Our teacher had a friend come to see her in school today."

"Charles's mother?" my husband and I asked simultaneously.

"Naaah," Laurie said scornfully. "It was a man who came and made us do exercises; we had to touch our toes. Look." He climbed down from his chair and squatted down and touched his toes. "Like this," he said. He got solemnly back into his chair and said, picking up his fork, "Charles didn't even *do* exercises."

"That's fine," I said heartily. "Didn't Charles want to do exercises?"

"Naaah," Laurie said. "Charles was so fresh to the teacher's friend he wasn't *let* do exercises."

"Fresh again?" I said.

"He kicked the teacher's friend," Laurie said. "The teacher's friend told Charles to touch his toes like I just did and Charles kicked him."

"What are they going to do about Charles, do you suppose?" Laurie's father asked him.

Laurie shrugged elaborately. "Throw him out of school, I guess," he said.

Wednesday and Thursday were routine; Charles yelled during story hour and hit a boy in the stomach and made him cry. On Friday Charles stayed after school again and so did all the other children.

With the third week
of kindergarten Charles
was an institution in our
family; the baby was being
a Charles when she cried
all afternoon; Laurie did
a Charles when he filled his
wagon full of mud and pulled it
through the kitchen; even my husband,
when he caught his elbow in the telephone cord and
pulled telephone, ashtray, and a bowl of flowers off the
table, said, after the first minute, "Looks like Charles."

During the third and fourth weeks it looked like a
reformation in Charles; Laurie reported grimly at lunch
on Thursday of the third week, "Charles was so good
today the teacher gave him an apple."

"What?" I said, and my husband added warily, "You
mean Charles?"

"Charles," Laurie said. "He gave the crayons around
and he picked up the books afterward and the teacher
said he was her helper."

"What happened?" I asked incredulously.

"He was her helper, that's all," Laurie said, and
shrugged.

"Can this be true, about Charles?" I asked my husband that night. "Can something like this happen?"

"Wait and see," my husband said cynically. "When
you've got a Charles to deal with, this may mean he's
only plotting."

18

He seemed to be wrong. For over a week Charles was the teacher's helper; each day he handed things out and he picked things up; no one had to stay after school.

"The PTA meeting's next week again," I told my husband one evening. "I'm going to find Charles's mother there."

"Ask her what happened to Charles," my husband said. "I'd like to know."

"I'd like to know myself," I said.

On Friday of that week things were back to normal. "You know what Charles did today?" Laurie demanded at the lunch table, in a voice slightly awed. "He told a little girl to say a word and she said it and the teacher washed her mouth out with soap and Charles laughed."

"What word?" his father asked unwisely, and Laurie said, "I'll have to whisper it to you, it's so bad." He got down off his chair and went around to his father. His father bent his head down and Laurie whispered joyfully. His father's eyes widened.

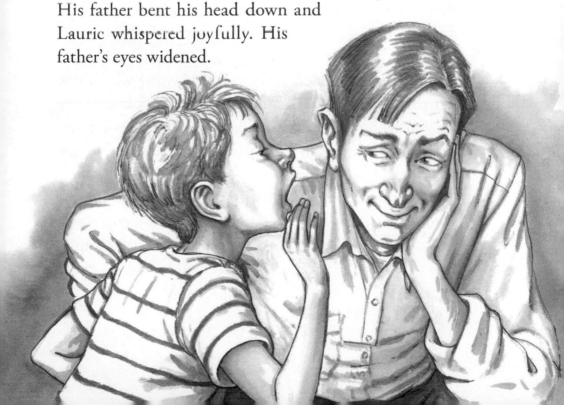

"Did Charles tell the little girl to say *that*?" he asked respectfully.

"She said it *twice*," Laurie said. "Charles told her to say it *twice*."

"What happened to Charles?" my husband asked.

"Nothing," Laurie said. "He was passing out the crayons."

Monday morning Charles abandoned the little girl and said the evil word himself three or four times, getting his mouth washed out with soap each time. He also threw chalk.

My husband came to the door with me that evening as I set out for the PTA meeting. "Invite her over for a cup of tea after the meeting," he said. "I want to get a look at her."

"If only she's there," I said prayerfully.

"She'll be there," my husband said. "I don't see how they could hold a PTA meeting without Charles's mother."

At the meeting I sat restlessly, scanning each comfortable matronly face, trying to determine which one hid the secret of Charles. None of them looked to me haggard enough. No one stood up in the meeting and apologized for the way her son had been acting. No one mentioned Charles.

After the meeting I identified and sought out Laurie's kindergarten teacher. She had a plate with a cup of tea and a piece of chocolate cake; I had a plate with a cup of tea and a piece of marshmallow cake. We maneuvered up to one another cautiously and smiled.

"I've been so anxious to meet you," I said. "I'm Laurie's mother."

"We're all so interested in Laurie," she said.

"Well, he certainly likes kindergarten," I said. "He talks about it all the time."

"We had a little trouble adjusting, the first week or so," she said primly, "but now he's a fine little helper. With occasional lapses, of course."

"Laurie usually adjusts very quickly," I said. "I suppose this time it's Charles's influence."

"Charles?"

"Yes," I said, laughing, "you must have your hands full in that kindergarten, with Charles."

"Charles?" she said. "We don't have any Charles in the kindergarten."

Her and me had to hotfoot it out of town.

THE SPECIAL POWERS
OF BLOSSOM CULP

Richard Peck

My name is Blossom Culp, and I'm ten years old, to the best of my mama's recollection.

I call 1900 the year of my birth, but Mama claims to have no idea of the day. Mama doesn't hold with birthdays. She says they make her feel old. This also saves her giving me a present. You could go through the courthouse down at Sikeston, Missouri, with a fine-tooth comb without turning up my records. But I must have been born because here I am.

Since Mama is hard to overlook, I will just mention her now. She doesn't know her birthday either but claims to be twenty-nine years old. She has only three teeth in her head, but they are up front so they make a good showing. Her inky hair flows over her bent shoulders and far down her back. Whenever she appeared in daylight down at Sikeston, horses reared. Mama is a sight.

But she is a woman of wisdom, and wonderful when it comes to root mixtures, forbidden knowledge, and other people's poultry. We could live off the land, though the trouble is, it's always somebody else's land. Like many of nature's creatures, Mama goes about her work at night. Get your corn in early, or Mama will have our share. Plant your tomatoes up by the house, or Mama will take them off you by the bushel. She likes her eggs fresh, too.

A moonless night suits her best, then off she goes down the hedgerows with a croaker sack flung over her humped shoulder. But nobody's ever caught her. "I can outrun a dawg," says Mama.

It was another of her talents that got us chased out of Sikeston. To hear her tell it, Mama has the Second Sight. For ready money she'll tell your fortune, find lost articles, see through walls, and call up the departed. She can read tea leaves, a pack of cards, your palm, a crystal ball. It doesn't matter to Mama. But because Sikeston was a backward place and narrow in its thinking, her profession was against the law. So her and me had to hotfoot it out of town two jumps ahead of a sheriff's posse.

Mama said that fate was mysteriously leading her to our next home place. But we'd have hopped a freight in any direction. Aboard a swaying cattle car, Mama grew thoughtful and pulled on her long chin.

"The farther north we get," she said, "the more progressive. Wherever we light, you'll be goin' to school." She shifted a plug of Bull Durham from one cheek to

the other. If Mama had ever been to school herself, she'd
have mentioned it. About all she can read is tea leaves.

"I been to school before, Mama," I reminded her.
Down at Sikeston, I'd dropped into the grade school
occasionally. Though when I dropped out again, I
wasn't missed.

"I mean you'll be goin' to school regular," Mama
said. "I don't want the law on me—believe it."

So when at last we came to rest at the town of Bluff
City, I knew school was in my future without even a
glimpse into Mama's crystal ball. I well recall the day
I strolled into the Horace Mann School in Bluff City,
wearing the same duds from when me and Mama had
dropped off a cattle car of the Wabash Railroad.

"Yewww," said many of the girls in the schoolyard,
giving me a wide berth. It was no better inside. I was
sent to the office of the principal before I had time to
break a rule. She was a woman tall as a tree named Miss
Mae Spaulding.

"Oh dear," she said, looking down at me, "we're going to have to find you a comb."

I was small for ten but old for my years. Miss Spaulding seemed to grasp this and assigned me to fourth grade. She took me there herself, shooing me on ahead like a chicken. The teacher, name of Miss Cartwright, took a gander at me and said, "Oh my stars."

"Perhaps you'd have a spare handkerchief to loan Blossom," the principal said to Miss Cartwright over my head.

I wiped my nose on my sleeve and noticed all the eyes of fourth grade were boring holes in me. The boys' eyes were round with amazement. The girls' eyes were mean slits.

"I guess we had better find Blossom a seat," Miss Cartwright said as Miss Spaulding beat a retreat out the door.

A big girl reared up out of her desk. She wore a bow the size of a kite on the back of her head. "She'll not be sitting next to me!" she sang out, and flopped back.

Her name turned out to be Letty Shambaugh, and once again I didn't need Mama's Second Sight to see I had met an enemy for life.

Miss Cartwright cleared her throat and said, "Boys and girls, we have a new class member. I will ask her to introduce herself."

I looked down the rows of fourth grade, and they looked capable of anything. Still, I stood my ground.

"My name is Blossom Culp," I said, "and I hail from down at Sikeston, Missouri."

Letty Shambaugh twitched in her seat. "Hillbillies," she hissed to the girls around her, "or worse."

"Me and Mama have relocated to Bluff City on account of her business," I said.

"Ah," says Miss Cartwright behind me, "and what . . . business is your mother engaged in?"

"Oh well shoot," I says, "my mama is well known for her herbal cures and fortune-telling. She can heal warts, too. There's gypsy blood in our family."

Letty Shambaugh smirked and so did all the girls around her. "Ah," says Miss Cartwright. "And are you an only child, Blossom?"

"I am now," I said. "I was born one-half of a pair of Siamese twins, but my twin had to be hacked off my side so I alone could live."

"She lies!" Letty Shambaugh called out, though all the boys were interested in my story.

By now Miss Cartwright had pulled back to the blackboard and seemed to be clinging to the chalk tray. "You may take your seat, Blossom." She pointed to the rear of the room.

I didn't mind it on the back row, but as the weeks passed, the novelty of going to school every day wore thin. My reading wasn't up to fourth-grade standard either. Still, when we had to rise and read aloud from a library book, I did right well. Holding a book before me, I'd tell a story I made up on the spot.

"Lies, lies," Letty would announce, "nothing but lies!" Still, Miss Cartwright was often so fascinated, she didn't stop me.

Then one day she told us that Letty would be having her birthday party on school time. "It is not usual to have a birthday party in class," Miss Cartwright said, "but we are making an exception of Letty."

People were always making an exception of Letty, and her paw was the president of the Board of Education. "Mrs. Shambaugh has very kindly offered to provide a cake," Miss Cartwright said, "and ice-cream punch."

At recess that day I was in the girls' rest room, which has partitions for modesty. From my stall I eavesdropped on Letty talking to the bunch of girls she rules: Tess and Bess, the Beasley twins; Nola Nirider; and Maisie Markham.

"Now shut up and listen," Letty told them. "I am looking for some first-rate presents from you-all for my birthday. Don't get me any of that five-and-dime stuff."

I was so interested in Letty's commandments that I leaned on the door of my stall and staggered out into full view.

"Oh there you are, Blossom," Letty sniffed. "Since you do nothing but tell lies and snoop, I'll thank you not to give me a present at all. You are a poor girl and can't afford it. Besides, I want nothing from the likes of you."

The bell rang, and they all flounced off like a gaggle of geese. But Letty turned back to fire a final warning. "And don't let me catch you spying on us again, Blossom."

You won't, I said, but only to myself.

I sat up that night, waiting for Mama to come home. We'd taken up residence in an abandoned structure over past the streetcar tracks. It must have been midnight before Mama came in and eased her croaker sack down.

Then she busied herself shaking out everything she'd harvested from nearby gardens. From the look of some of it, she'd detoured past the town dump. It was late in the season, so all there was to eat was a handful of pale parsnips.

"Well, Mama, I've got me a problem," I told her. "A stuck-up girl at school is having a birthday party, and I mean to give her a present like anybody else."

Mama surveyed her night's haul. "See anything here you can use?"

She held up a lady's whalebone corset straight off the trash heap and busted beyond repair. Besides, it wouldn't go halfway around Letty. The rest of the stuff was worse, except for a nice hatbox only a little dented with the tissue paper still inside. I reached for it. Mama only shrugged, picking between two of her three teeth.

The school days droned on, but I kept my wits about me. In one of my read-alouds, I went too far. Holding up a library copy of *Rebecca of Sunnybrook Farm*, I told the class about the time my mama came across the severed head of a woman and how Mama could identify the murderer with her Second Sight.

"A pack of lies!" Letty bawled out, "and disgusting."

"That will do, Blossom," Miss Cartwright said in a weary voice. So after that, I had little to occupy myself with but to lie low and snoop on other people's business.

On the afternoon of Letty's party, a cake was wheeled in as large and pink as Letty herself. The classroom was stacked with tastefully wrapped presents, and no

learning was done in fourth grade that afternoon. Miss Cartwright hung at the edge while Letty was the center of attention, where she likes to be.

We played some games too childish to interest me, but I managed three slabs of cake and copped an extra slice to take home to Mama. Then it was time for the presents.

"Oh heavens, you shouldn't have!" says Letty, her pudgy fingers fluttering over the vast heap. "Land sakes, I don't know which one to open first."

"Start with this one." I nudged the hatbox toward her with the toe of my shoe. I'd dressed it up with a bow I found in the school yard and some gold star stickers I'd come across in a teacher's desk.

Miss Cartwright was standing by. Though strict, she sometimes eyed me sympathetically, though it might only have been pity. "Yes, Letty," she said. "Start with Blossom's present."

So Letty had to. She shook the box but heard nothing. She lifted off the lid and ran a hand through the tissue paper. "But there's nothing in it!" she gasped, shooting me a dangerous look.

Some of the boys snickered, but the girls just pursed up their lips. "Oh dear," Miss Cartwright remarked. Now Letty had turned the hatbox upside down. The tissue paper dropped out and with it a small note I'd hand lettered. She read it aloud:

> To Letty,
>   Since I am too poor to buy you a present,
> I will share with you my own personal Gift.
>   Believe it,
>
> Blossom Culp

Letty glanced longingly at her other presents. "What is this so-called personal Gift of yours, Blossom?"

"Just a little demonstration of the Special Powers I inherited from my mama," I replied.

Letty shook a fist at me. "Blossom, you aren't going to ruin my party by showing off and telling lies!"

"For example," I said, cool as a cucumber, "before you even open up your other presents, I can tell what's in them with my Inner Eye. It's a Gift, and I have it down pat."

The girls were about to turn on me, but a boy said, "Then do it."

I could read the card on Nola Nirider's. "Now you take Nola's present." I pointed it out. "No, I don't want to touch it. Just give me a minute." I let my head loll. Then I let my eyes roll back in my head. It was a ghastly sight, and the class gasped. In a voice faint and far-off I said, "Within the wrappings, I see . . . a woman! She is a dainty creature cut in two at the waist!" I let my eyes roll back in place and looked around. "What did I say?"

Letty was already tearing open Nola's present. She pulled out a dainty china powder box in the shape of a lady. It was in two parts. The lid was the upper half. The boys blinked, and the girls looked worried.

Reading the card on Maisie's present from afar, I said, "Now you take that one from Maisie Markham." And back flipped my eyes, and my head bobbed around till it like to fall off. "Deep within that fancy package," I moaned weirdly, "is a sealed bottle of apple-blossom

toilet water—retailing at seventy-nine cents. I sense it with my Inner Nose."

Letty ripped open the box, coming up with that self-same bottle of toilet water. "How am I doin'?" I asked the class.

It was the same with Tess's brush-and-comb set and Bess's four hair ribbons in rainbow hues. My eyes rolled back so often, showing my whites, that I thought I'd never get them straight in their sockets.

By now Letty sat sprawled in a heap of wrapping paper, the tears starting down her red face. She was clouding up and ready to squall and had to stand up to stamp her foot. "You have ruined my party with your showing off, Blossom. I knew you would, and you have!" She pounded out of the room before she even got to any presents from the boys, which was just as well. The other girls followed her out as usual.

It's true. I stole Letty's thunder and her party, too. Now I was left with the boys, who showed me new respect, unsure of my special powers. But then the bell rang, and they trooped out, taking final swipes at the remains of the birthday cake.

"One moment, Blossom," Miss Cartwright said before I could make it to the door. "Could it be as you say—that you have . . . unearthly powers? Or could it merely be that you eavesdropped in the restroom often enough to hear those girls telling each other what they were giving Letty—and then you added that business with your eyes?"

Her chalky hand rested on my shoulder. "No, don't tell me," she said. "I don't want to know."

I was ready to go, but Miss Cartwright continued. "It has not taken you long to make a name for yourself at Horace Mann School. You will never be popular. But I have hopes for your future, Blossom. You will go far in your own peculiar way."

And I only nodded, as it's never wise to disagree with a teacher. Then she turned me loose, and I went on my way.

Shnook was different.

THE PEDDLER'S GIFT

Maxine Rose Schur

In Korovenko, late summer was hot and damp. The rye grew high as corn, the air smelled of fallen plums, and near our thatched-roof hut the river babbled all day like a happy baby.

But in all this warm beauty there was little time for play. From sunrise to sunset we boys studied Torah, and after that it was supper, prayers, and bed. On Shabbos we rested and strolled through the plum orchards at the edge of the village. Only on Wednesday, when our school let out early, did we get a chance to run, yell, play Cossacks, and swish our bare feet in the tickle-cold waters of the river.

One Wednesday afternoon my friend Moshe and I were making swords from fallen oak branches, when he asked, "Leibush, have you seen Shnook?"

"What?" I cried. "Is Shnook here?"

"Sure. He arrived from Pinsk last night and slept in the synagogue. Yankel saw his wagon there this morning."

"Maybe he'll come to our house again!" I yelled, jumping up. "Maybe he's there now!" Grabbing my sword, I ran up the riverbank toward home. Every peddler who happened through our village brought merriment, but Shnook brought more laughs than any of them.

Lucky me. There at the side of our hut was his broken-down cart. I opened the door and saw my father and the peddler sitting at our table, drinking glasses of tea. Standing between them, my mother cut two large slices of her honey cake. The peddler chewed the cake slowly. His face was thin and dry, and his hands were bony and rough from driving his wagon. His smile was warm, yet he spoke so little, my father once said his words must be weighed, not counted. Shimon was the peddler's real name, but because he seemed a simpleton, the children of Korovenko called him Shnook.

Now Shnook stood up and in his meek voice said, "Please come and see what I have." As I edged closer, he glanced at me, then smiled at my father. "Your boy has grown taller," he said.

"Yes." Papa beamed. "In summer Leibush shoots up like a wildflower."

Shnook smiled at me for several moments, and despite my feeling that he must be a noodle-head, I smiled back.

Some of the older boys said Shnook was not just simple, but bad. They believed he had been put under a spell by the Evil Eye, and that's why he bungled things. Yankel even said Shnook had magic powers and could use certain words to trick you, make you forget your name, cause feathers to sprout from your ears and little stewing onions to grow between your toes. I didn't know what to believe. Papa had many times warned me against gossip. He told me what I didn't see with my eyes not to make up with my mouth. And yet surely this peddler from Pinsk was cut from a different cloth than the other peddlers who traveled through our village.

Other peddlers opened their great bags with a flourish, waved their arms, and smiled like fathers at a wedding as they described their wares in long flowery words.

"Good Jewish wife," they would exclaim, "allow me please to show you the most excellent of stew pots! Here I have, just for your inspection, direct from the fiery kilns of St. Petersburg, a silver-toned tin pot fit for a fat goose at the banquet of the czar, may a thunderbolt strike his head!"

After noisy bargaining, other peddlers would stay for a glass of tea, and then another, a cookie, a slice of honey cake, and more often than not, a supper of soup and groats.

And when the oil lamps were lit, these peddlers who drove from Moscow to Minsk wove tales of intrigue about the czar's court. The whole world lay on their tongues. They brought news from Kiev and Vladivostok. They described the fashions of the cities to the merriment of the women, all the while pinching the cheeks of the youngest children and slipping cinnamon candies into their small hands.

But Shnook was different.

The villagers said that if Shnook sold coffins, people would stop dying. The truth was, nothing he did turned out right. One time he left his goods in Pinsk and traveled to Rovno with an empty bag. Another time he left his bag open near a kitchen door where a goat was tied up. The goat ate five pairs of socks and a hat. Still another time he sold all his wares to himself, then gave them to a poor family.

There's a saying: "When a foolish buyer goes to market, the sellers rejoice." But in Korovenko when Shnook the Peddler arrived, the buyers rejoiced! If someone actually expressed interest in his goods,

he might exclaim, "Nu? You really want to buy these handkerchiefs? The cloth is thin and the stitching poor. It's better you keep your money."

Worse yet, Shnook had no idea how to buy goods from the wholesalers. He would often end up with such odd things, even he did not know what they were. Once he mistakenly sold shoehorns as spatulas, and another time he bought three hundred fountain pens—all of them leaking. Schnook has such bad luck, people joked, even his fountain pens cry!

Now, as we all watched, he opened his ragged leather bag. He took his goods out so silently, you would have thought he was hiding them rather than presenting them for sale. He carefully laid out red silk ribbons, boxes of matches, small glass bottles of rose water, great flag-sized squares of cloth, embroidered pillowcases, painted wooden spoons, writing paper and jars of black ink, bone and wood buttons, paper-wrapped packages of needles, brass buttonhooks, pure white cakes of soap nesting in blue tissue, and lace tablecloths all the way from Hungary.

When he came to the religious items, he showed special care. On the table he gently placed Shabbos bread covers, prayer shawls, Shabbos candles, and my favorite, the four-sided Hanukkah tops we called dreidels. Shnook's dreidels were big. They were fist-sized, hand-carved from birch wood, and could spin nearly three minutes without falling!

We gazed wide-eyed at all the glorious new things that transformed our soot-stained hut into a colorful bazaar. Even Papa, who took little notice of such things, looked amazed.

The peddler stood back and stared down at his boots as if discovering two old friends. He always seemed shy when showing his goods, so waited for my mother to make the first move.

My mother, never wishing to cause him discomfort, began to look over the goods, touching many of the items gently, thinking to herself about each one. I watched while she stroked the heavy cotton fabric from Zhitomir. It was deep blue, the color of cornflowers, and I knew my mother would have dearly loved to buy it—to sew it, to dress me up like a scholar. But we were not for that sort of thing. My trousers were made from my father's old ones. My shirt was cut from Mama's discarded dress. Even my jacket had lived a former life as Uncle Solly's coat.

Mama never had more to spend than one ruble, and this time she chose matches, writing paper, and the Shabbos candles. When she had selected her purchases, she asked how much they cost, and the magic was that the peddler always said, "One ruble."'

Mama sighed and handed Shnook the ruble. It was then, while he was writing out the receipt, I noticed one of the dreidels under the chair. As he gathered his wares, he did not see the fallen dreidel. I should have picked it up for him, but something inside me froze. I stood in front of the chair, reasoning frantically. He won't miss it; after all, he never notices anything. Besides, I'll just borrow it, and the next time he comes to town, I'll find a way to slip it back to him.

Just then my father's voice interrupted my thoughts. "Shimon, the sky is dark now, and the air is heavy. We would be honored if you would share our supper with us and stay the night."

As always, Shnook made an excuse to go. "Thank you, but Pinsk is still two days away, and I want to get there by Shabbos."

"But, Shimon," my mother asked, "where will you go if it rains?"

The peddler opened the door. "There is my shelter," he said. "My carpet is the road; my ceiling, the sky; and my lamps, the stars."

That night after prayers, I climbed onto my bed above the warm brick oven and listened to the crashing sound of the late summer storm. I had hidden the dreidel under my feather bed, and now I took it out to feel its smooth wood in the dark. My parents had fallen asleep quickly, but I could not sleep. They say a thief has an easy job but difficult dreams. My mind spun like a dreidel as I imagined being in jail, laughed at and scorned. "There is Leibush, the thief, the thief, the thief." I saw my father, my mother, the rabbi, all the villagers pointing at me while the dreidel burned in my hand. Outside, the rain pounded down as if it were crying for me, while nightmarish images stormed through my head. Then suddenly I saw the trusting face of the peddler and realized with a terrible certainty that I had done wrong.

In the dark I laced up my boots and put on my coat. Tucking the dreidel into the pocket, I slipped out into the rain.

I ran through the village, heading for the synagogue, for I hoped if Shnook would be in any dry place tonight,

he would be there. The night was wild. In the black sky, ghostly clouds traveled quickly across the heavens. The wind howled like a dog in pain, and the rain beat down so angrily that the twisted cobblestone streets were changed into rivers.

Lights were on in the synagogue. I peeked through the side window but it streamed with rain, and I could see only someone's shadow. I went to the door and found it slightly open. I had straight in my mind what I was going to say to him. I would confess my sin right away and give back the dreidel. Then I would ask him to forgive me. I trembled as I entered the synagogue, partly from the cold but mostly from fear. An oil lamp burned brightly. I walked in, the rain dripping off me, forming small puddles on the floor. Suddenly I heard singing in a voice so strong and beautiful, I couldn't move. The peddler was not here! Someone else, some powerful-voiced traveler had sought shelter in the synagogue tonight. My disappointment was so great, I began to cry.

The man broke off his splendid song and walked toward me. His face was bright with such happiness that at first I did not recognize him.

"Leibush!" he said. "What are you doing here on this terrible night?"

His words startled me. For a few horrible seconds I had forgotten why I was there and could do nothing but cry. At last my tears stopped, and I said through chattering teeth, "I came to bring you this. You left it in our home." I handed him the dreidel. "I mean . . . I stole it." Shnook pulled a handkerchief from his pocket and wiped my face.

"Come," he beckoned, getting dry clothes from his valise. "Change your clothes."

After I had changed, the storm was still raging, so Shnook insisted I remain in the synagogue until it passed. He wrapped himself in his coat and made me sleep on his feather quilt. As we bedded down, I said, "I'm sorry I took your dreidel."

"I know you are," was all he replied.

"But why aren't you angry with me?" I asked.

He looked at me for a few seconds, smoothing his beard. "First of all," he said with a small smile, "I knew you had taken it."

"You knew!"

"I saw you put it in your pocket. Thank the Lord, you are not a good thief!"

"You knew . . . and still you're not angry! Why aren't you angry?" For some reason my own voice had anger in it.

"We are in the Lord's house. There is too much peace here to be angry. You were angry at yourself. That is what really mattered."

The peddler pulled the coat tighter around him. It was too short to cover his feet, and I saw his worn socks dotted with holes.

When we woke, it was still dark. After dressing and praying, he hitched Fresser to

his cart and said good-bye. In that gray, dead world that exists before dawn, I watched the peddler steer his old cart down the mud-washed road toward Pinsk.

I turned homeward. My sleeping village lay cold and wet around me, giving off the odor of damp wood and musty hay. I reached home before my parents woke, and climbed back into bed.

Though he returned to Korovenko for many years, I never again called him Shnook. He was Shimon, the Peddler from Pinsk. Shimon the wise, the strong, the kind. The one who left cotton the color of cornflowers by our door, and on Hanukkah a big, birch-carved dreidel.

I have it to this day.

On snowy Hanukkah nights, when the candles burn short and the dreidel spins its lone path across the landscape of our floor, I see him traveling to Pinsk. His carpet, the road; his ceiling, the sky; and his lamps, the stars.

Theme Introduction

Self-Respect

In this section of the book, you will read about characters who face challenges to their self-respect. Thinking about these stories, and about your own experiences with self-respect, will give you new ideas about what it means to respect yourself.

IMPORTANT QUESTIONS TO THINK ABOUT

Before starting this section, think about your own experiences with self-respect:

- What makes you proud to be who you are?
- Has thinking about your self-respect ever affected a decision you have made?

Once you have thought about your own experiences with self-respect, think about this **theme question** and write down your answers or share them aloud:

What does it mean to respect yourself?

After reading each story in this section, ask yourself the theme question again. You may have some new ideas you want to add.

Twi loved Mentu like her own soul.

In the Time of the Drums

Gullah folktale
as told by Kim L. Siegelson

In the long ago time before now, on an island fringed by marsh meadows and washed by ocean tides, men and women and their children lived enslaved. This was the time when giant live oaks trembled with the sound of drums, and, say some, it was a time when people could walk beneath the water.

Used to be, in those early days, ships as big as barns would land at a dock on a bluff near Teakettle Creek: pirate ships with treasure to bury, cargo ships filled with cinnamon, slave ships bringing African people to do work on plantation farms.

Some of those Africans came knowing how to carve wood and make sweet-grass baskets and goatskin drums.

With those things they reminded themselves of home. Wished to go back there.

One boy, name of Mentu, had never known Africa or longed for it. He was an island-born boy.

Mentu could scoot to the top of a live oak faster than a brush-tail squirrel. Could lift a black iron skillet above his head with one hand, even though he still wore shirttails. "Look how strong I am!" he would say to his grandmother, Twi.

Twi would smile back and cluck her tongue at him. "Stop your foolin' lest the overseer catch you, sir. Your time for strong will come soon enough."

"When?" Mentu would ask. Twi would not say.

Mentu had always lived with Twi. The islanders, black and white, all feared her.

Africa had been her birthplace.

There, she had learned powerful root magic at her own grandmother's knee. "Ibo conjure woman," the islanders called her. "Older than anyone living," they said.

But Mentu paid them no mind, had only known kindness from Twi. You see, Twi loved Mentu like her own soul. Like the faraway rivers and mountains of her native land. Some said his first breath had come from her own mouth. That as a new babe he had been still until she whispered the secret of life onto his tongue. He had wailed at the truth of it and waved his fists at her, and at the charm bag she held out to him. "Not with fists," she had said, gathering him against her chest. "Listen close and learn how to be strong." He had slept to the sound of Twi's heart.

Every day Mentu went with Twi to take water to the fields. Could carry two full buckets by himself. Strong as that made him seem, he was a mischief-making boy-child all the same.

"The bucket handles pinch my hands," he sometimes complained to Twi. "You carry the water for me today."

"Nawsir!" she would say and cluck her tongue. "Twi can't be taking up your burden from you. Look out to the field workers when your hands is aching and count your luck. Soon it will be your time to be strong-strong, and Twi won't be helping you then."

"How will I know when to be strong-strong if you don't tell me?" Mentu asked.

Twi still would not answer. She knew many secrets. She shared only what she wanted.

Mentu looked to the fields and watched the people bend beneath the blistering sun to slave in soil planted with cotton and cane and blue indigo seed. Saw how they worked from dark of morning to dark of night, harvesting what they could not keep.

Twi told him that the long, hard work had broken them. Made memories of Africa sink so far back in their minds that they could no longer be reached. The old ways had slowly slipped away and been left behind like sweat drops in a newly plowed row.

But Twi remembered the time before.

Spoke the old words to herself in the morning while she worked. Sang African songs to Mentu in the afternoon until he could sing them back. At dinner, told him old stories so rich that he could almost smell the sweet-scented air of her homeland. Put the skin drum between her own knees and taught him ancient rhythms until they felt as natural to him as his own heart beating.

Then, come a day so hot even the gnats hushed their whining to sit among the tree shadows. In that breath-less quiet, Mentu and Twi filled their buckets with well water. But before they could carry them to the fields they heard the sound of drums beating from the far end of the island. *Bop-boom-boom! Bop-boom-boom!*

It was a message in rhythm that meant "A ship is come! A ship is come!"

Mentu beat his own drum. *Be-e-bow. Be-e-bow.* "We hear. We hear." He and

Twi gathered with everyone else at the bluff to see what the ship had brought. It flew a Spanish flag, but it did not carry gold or jewels or sweet spices from India. The ship held a whole village of Ibo people from the African kingdom of Benin. They had been captured by the ship's owners and brought to the island to be sold.

Their ride across the ocean passage had been long, with many days spent in airless dark beneath the pitching decks of the ship.

When the ship docked at the bluff, the Ibo people could no longer hear the crash of ocean waves—only the groan of the ship, the flapping sails, and their own harsh breathing. They trembled and waited quietly, listening to learn something of their fate. Through the wooden side of the ship came the sound of the island drums. The music of Africa.

"Has some magic brought us home?" they cried. They drummed an answer using their feet on the wooden floor.

Mentu heard the rumble of their pounding feet, and it spoke to him like the beating of his heart. "We are home! We are home!" the people drummed. But they were far from home.

Mentu and Twi watched the Ibo people brought up from the dark hull of the ship into the light. Saw how they squinted into the sun. How they looked out over the unfamiliar marsh meadows in despair. The ship had not returned them to Africa. Would never take them home again.

Try as the ship's captain might to make them move, the Ibo people refused to set a foot on the island. Mentu turned away when the overseer lashed them with his whip. But the people would not budge for the whip. Just joined their hands tight together and began to chant a song in their own language.

Mentu listened as though his soul lived in his ears. He heard Twi's music in their song. Old words from the place where she had been born.

"What are they saying, Twi?" he asked. "Sounds like magic."

Twi's eyes glittered like moonsparkle on dark water. "Old magic long forgot, boy," she whispered. "The people want to go home. Say the water brought 'em cross the passage and it can take 'em back, fe true." She hung her charm bag around Mentu's neck. "That water can take me on, too, Mentu. You are old enough. Your time to be strong-strong is near."

Mentu began to tremble. "Will the water take me, Twi? I want to go with you."

His grandmother shook her head. "Water won't take you. You was born here. Won't take the others 'cause they've forgot too much."

"But you haven't taught me all your secrets, Twi," Mentu cried. "You haven't told me when my time will come yet."

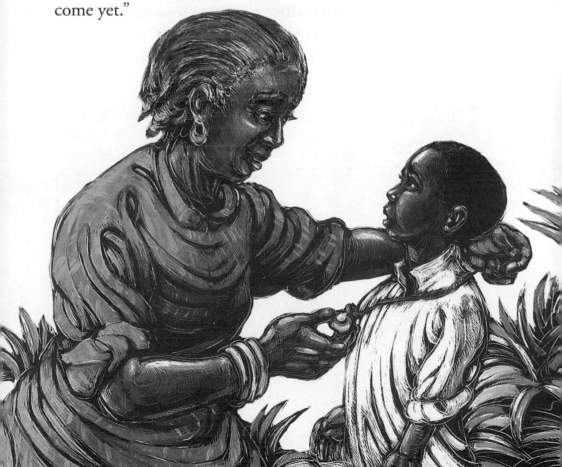

Twi clucked her tongue at him, still a mischief-making boy-child. "Twi has taught you many things, Mentu. More secrets than you think. But I will tell you one more. Your time to be strong-strong will come when your back is bent in the fields and your hands are stuck full of cotton spurs. Because then the old ways will try to grow weak inside you. Don't let 'em! Takes a mighty strength not to forget who you are. Where you come from. To help others remember it, too. Now I must leave you, my child, my heart."

Then Twi kissed Mentu fast as a dragonfly. Took off running. And as she ran, the years melted from her like butter on an ash cake. Her back drew up straight. Her hair grew dark and thick with braids, and her skin smoothed until she looked like the young woman who had been taken from Africa those many years before. The islanders feared Twi more than ever when they saw this happen, and they fell back to let her pass. No one tried to stop her.

From the bluff she held her hands out to the Ibo people on the dock and spoke to them. "Come with me, my brothers and sisters. I will take you home."

Mentu wept as the people crossed the dock to join the young Twi on the land. The slave catchers tried to slip ropes around their necks and arms to hold them back, but couldn't. The ropes slipped through flesh and bone like it was smoke and seawater.

Twi clasped hands with the Ibo people and led them down the bluff to the water's edge. "Twi!" Mentu called out to her, but she would not turn back, even for him.

She chanted as she led the people waist deep into the waters of Teakettle Creek. Mentu wiped away his tears and chanted with her in a voice as strong as he could make it, "The water can take us home. The water can take us home." He tried to run to her but found his feet fastened to the land so that he could not move.

Twi and the other Ibo people lifted their faces to the sky as water crept over their shoulders and then their necks. But they kept walking, as their chains snapped away. "The water can take us home," they sang. "It can take us home."

Their song dissolved into bubble and foam as Teakettle Creek swirled over the tops of their heads. Mentu's feet suddenly pulled away from the ground and he ran to the water, but he couldn't see Twi or the Ibo people beneath its surface.

In time, Mentu swore to everyone left behind that Twi and the Ibos had walked all the way back to Africa on the bottom of the ocean, pulling each other along the sandy floors, pushing aside seaweed like long grass.

"But their chains and their song will never leave Teakettle Creek," others said. "And the water there will always be salty as tears."

The islanders called that place Ibo's Landing. Stopped fishing there and never cast another net in Teakettle Creek for fear of pulling up those chains sunk deep in soft gray mud. Shivered when snowy egrets rose from the marsh grass like spirits in the evening.

As for Mentu, he learned to be strong-strong in the fields beneath the blistering sun, just as Twi had told him. He sang her old songs to himself while he worked and to his children until they could sing them back to him. He told stories so rich that they wondered if he had lived in Africa himself. And he played rhythms on the skin drum until they felt their own hearts beat in time. Gave them their own drums and they all played together, Mentu and his children.

And they taught their own children, and they taught theirs, through slave time and freedom time and on up until now time.

Fe true, it takes a mighty strength not to forget.

We were going to work, and not to school.

LEARNING THE GAME

Francisco Jiménez

I was in a bad mood. It was the last day of seventh grade before summer vacation. I had known the day was coming, but I had tried not to think about it because it made me sad. For my classmates, it was a happy day. During the afternoon, Miss Logan asked for volunteers to share what they were going to do during the summer; lots of hands went up. Some talked about going away on trips; others about summer camp. I folded my hands under the desk, lowered my head, and tried not to listen. After a while, I managed to tune out what they were saying and only heard faint voices coming from different parts of the room.

In the school bus on the way home, I took out my notepad and pencil from my shirt pocket and began figuring out how much time before I would start school again—from the middle of June until the first week of

November, about four and a half months. Ten weeks picking strawberries in Santa Maria and another eight weeks harvesting grapes and cotton in Fresno. As I added the number of days, I started to get a headache. Looking out the window I said to myself, "One-hundred-thirty-two more days after tomorrow."

As soon as I arrived home, I took two of Papá's aspirins and lay down. I had just closed my eyes when I heard Carlos, our neighbor, shouting outside. "Come on, Panchito, we're starting the game."

The game was kick-the-can. I played it with Carlos and my younger brothers, Trampita, Torito, and Rubén, on school days when I had no homework, and on weekends when I was not too tired from working in the fields.

"Hurry, or else!" Carlos hollered impatiently.

I liked the game, but I did not enjoy playing with Carlos. He was older than I, and often reminded me of it, especially when I disagreed with him. If we wanted to play, we had to follow his rules. No one could play unless he said so. He wore tight jeans and a white T-shirt with the sleeves rolled up to show off his muscles. Under his right sleeve, he tucked a cigarette pack.

"Come on Panchito!" Trampita yelled. "You're making us wait."

I went outside to play. I wanted to forget about the next 133 days.

"It's about time," Carlos said, giving me a light punch on the right shoulder. "You'll be the guard," he said, pointing at Rubén. "Trampita, you draw the circle.

Torito, you get the can." As Carlos was giving orders, I saw Manuelito standing by one of the garbage cans. During every game, he stood by himself on the sidelines because Carlos would not let him play. "Let Manuelito be the guard," I said to Carlos.

"No way," he responded annoyingly. "I already told you before, he can't play. He's too slow."

"Come on, Carlos, let him play," I insisted.

"No!" he shouted, giving me and Manuelito a dirty look.

"Go ahead and play, Panchito," Manuelito said timidly. "I'll stand here and watch."

We started the game, and the more we played, the less I thought about my troubles. Even my headache went away. We played until dark.

The alarm clock went off early the next morning. I glanced at the window. It was still dark outside. I shut my eyes, trying to get one more minute of sleep, but Roberto, my older brother, jumped out of bed and pulled off the covers. "Time to get up!" he said. When I saw him putting on his work clothes, I remembered we were going to work, and not to school. My shoulders felt heavy.

On the way to the fields, Papá turned on the *Carcachita's* headlights to see through the thick fog that blew in from the coast. It covered the valley every morning, like a large gray sheet. Ito, the sharecropper, was waiting for us when we arrived. Then a black pickup truck appeared. We could see it through the wall of fog, not far from where we parked. The driver stopped behind our *Carcachita* and, in perfect Spanish, ordered the passenger who rode in the bed of the truck to get off.

"Who's that?" I asked Papá, pointing to the driver.

"Don't point," Papá said. "It's bad manners. He's Mr. Díaz, the *contratista*. He runs the *bracero* camp for Sheehey Berry Farms. The man with him is one of the *braceros*."

In his broken Spanish, Ito introduced us to Gabriel, the man who accompanied the *contratista*.

Gabriel looked a few years older than Roberto.

He wore a pair of loose tan pants and a blue shirt. The shirt was faded. His straw hat was slightly tilted to the right, and he had long dark sideburns that were trimmed and came down to the middle of his square jaw. His face was weather-beaten. The deep cracks in the back of his heels were as black as the soles of his *huaraches*.

Gabriel took off his hat and we shook hands. He seemed nervous. But he relaxed when we greeted him in Spanish.

After the *contratista* left, we marched in line to the end of the field, selected a row, and started to work. Gabriel ended up between Papá and me. Because it was Gabriel's first time harvesting strawberries, Ito asked Papá to show him how to pick. "It's easy, Don Gabriel," Papá said. "The main thing is to make sure

the strawberry is ripe and not bruised or rotten. And when you get tired from squatting, you can pick on your knees." Gabriel learned quickly by watching and following Papá.

At noon, Papá invited Gabriel to join us for lunch in our *Carcachita*. He sat next to me in the back seat while Roberto and Papá sat in the front. From his brown paper bag, he pulled out a Coke and three sandwiches: one of mayonnaise and two of jelly. "Not again! We get this same lunch from that Díaz every day," he complained. "I am really tired of this."

"You can have one of my *taquitos*," I said.

"Only if you take this jelly sandwich," he responded, handing it to me. I looked at Papá's face. When I saw him smile, I took it and thanked him.

"Do you have a family, Don Gabriel?" Papá asked.

"Yes, and I miss them a lot," he answered. "Especially my three kids."

"How old are they?" Papá asked.

"The oldest is five, the middle one is three, and the little one, a girl, is two. And you, Don Pancho, how many do you have?"

"A handful," Papá answered, grinning. "Five boys and a girl. All living at home."

"You're lucky. You get to see them every day," Gabriel said. "I haven't seen mine for months." He continued as though thinking out loud. "I didn't want to leave them, but I had no choice. We have to eat, you know. I send them a few dollars every month for food and things. I'd like to send them more, but after I pay Díaz for room and board and transportation, little is left." Then in an angry tone of voice he added, "Díaz is a crook. He over-charges for everything. That *sin vergüenza* doesn't know who he's dealing with."

At this point, we heard the honking of a car horn. It was Ito signaling us that it was time to go back to work. Our half-hour lunch break was over.

That evening, and for several days after, I was too tired to play outside when we got home from work. I went straight to bed after supper. But as I got more and more used to picking strawberries, I began to play kick-the-can again. The game was always the same. We played by Carlos's rules, and he refused to let Manuelito play.

Work was always the same, too. We picked from six o'clock in the morning until six in the afternoon. Even though the days were long, I looked forward to seeing Gabriel and having lunch with him every day. I enjoyed listening to him tell stories and talk about Mexico. He was as proud of being from the state of Morelos as my father was about being from Jalisco.

One Sunday, near the end of the strawberry season, Ito sent me to work for a sharecropper who was sick and needed extra help that day. His field was next to Ito's. Gabriel was loaned out to the same farmer. As soon as I arrived, the *contratista* began giving me orders. "Listen, *hüerquito*, I want you to hoe weeds. But first, give me and Gabriel a hand," he said. Gabriel and I climbed onto the bed of the truck and helped him unload a plow. The *contratista* tied one end of a thick rope to it and, handing the other end to Gabriel, said, "Here, tie this around your waist. I want you to till the furrows."

"I can't do that," Gabriel said with a painful look on his face.

"What do you mean you can't?" responded the *contratista*, placing his hands on his hips.

"In my country, oxen pull plows, not men," Gabriel replied, tilting his hat back. "I am not an animal."

The *contratista* walked up to Gabriel and yelled in his face, "Well this isn't your country, idiot! You either do what I say or I'll have you fired!"

"Don't do that, please," Gabriel said. "I have a family to feed."

"I don't give a damn about your family!" the *contratista* replied, grabbing Gabriel by the shirt collar and pushing him. Gabriel lost his balance and fell backward. As he hit the ground, the *contratista* kicked him in the side with the tip of his boot. Gabriel sprung up and, with both hands clenched, lunged at the *contratista*. White as a ghost, Díaz quickly jumped back. "Don't be stupid . . . your family," he stammered. Gabriel held back. His face was flushed with rage. Without taking his eyes off Gabriel, the *contratista* slid into his truck and sped off, leaving us in a cloud of dust.

I felt scared. I had not seen men fight before. My mouth felt dry and my hands and legs began to shake. Gabriel threw his hat on the ground and said angrily, "That Díaz is a coward. He thinks he's a big man because he runs the *bracero* camp for the growers. He's nothing but a leech! And now he tries to treat me like an animal. I've had it." Then, picking up his hat and putting it on, he added, "He can cheat me out of my money. He can fire me. But he can't force me to do what isn't right. He can't take away my dignity. That he can't do!"

All day, while Gabriel and I hoed weeds, I kept thinking about what happened that morning. It made me angry and sad. Gabriel cursed as he hacked at the weeds.

When I got home from work that evening, I felt restless. I went outside to play kick-the-can. "Come on guys, let's play!" Carlos yelled out, resting his right foot on the can.

I went up to Manuelito, who was sitting on the ground and leaning against one of the garbage cans. "You heard Carlos, let's play," I said loudly so that Carlos could hear me.

"He didn't mean me," Manuelito answered, slowly getting up.

"Yes, you too," I insisted.

"Is it true, Carlos?" Manuelito asked.

"No way!" Carlos shouted.

Manuelito put his hands in his pockets and walked away.

"If Manuelito doesn't play, I won't either," I said. As soon as I said it, my heart started pounding. My knees felt weak. Carlos came right up to me. He had fire in his eyes. "Manuelito doesn't play!" he yelled.

He stuck his right foot behind my feet and pushed me. I fell flat on my back. My brothers rushed over to help me up. "You can push me around, but you can't force me to play!" I yelled back, dusting off my clothes and walking away. Trampita, Torito, Rubén, and Manuelito followed me to the front of our barrack.

Carlos stood alone inside the circle in the dirt, looking at the can and glancing at us once in a while. After a few moments, he cocked his head back, spat on the ground, and swaggered toward us saying, "Okay, Manuelito can play."

Screaming with joy, Manuelito and my brothers jumped up and down like grasshoppers. I felt like celebrating, too, but I held back. I did not want Carlos to see how happy I was.

The following morning, when Ito told us that the *contratista* had gotten Gabriel fired and sent back to Mexico, I felt like someone had kicked me in the stomach. I could not concentrate on work. At times I found myself not moving at all. By the time I had picked one crate, Papá had picked two. He finished his row, started a second, and caught up to me.

"What's the matter, Panchito?" he asked. "You're moving too slow. You need to speed it up."

"I keep thinking about Gabriel," I answered.

"What Díaz did was wrong, and someday he'll pay for it, if not in this life, in the next one," he said. "Gabriel did what he had to do."

Papá pushed me along, handing me several handfuls of strawberries he picked from my row. With his help, I got through that long day.

When we got home from work, I did not want to play kick-the-can. I wanted to be alone, but my brothers would not let me. They followed me around, asking me to play.

I finally gave in when Manuelito came over and joined them. "Please, just one game," he pleaded.

"Okay, just one," I answered.

We drew sticks to see who would play guard. Carlos was it. While he counted to twenty with his eyes closed, we ran and hid. I went behind a pepper tree that was next to the outhouse. When Carlos spotted me, he shouted, "I spy Panchito!" We both raced to the can. I got to it first and kicked it with all my might. It went up in the air and landed in one of the garbage cans. That was the last time I played the game.

"I believe she wants to be invisible for a while."

THE INVISIBLE CHILD

Tove Jansson

One dark and rainy evening the Moomin family sat around the veranda table picking over the day's mushroom harvest. The big table was covered with newspapers, and in the center of it stood the lighted kerosene lamp. But the corners of the veranda were dark.

"My has been picking pepper spunk again," Moominpappa said. "Last year she collected flybane."

"Let's hope she takes to chanterelles next autumn," said Moominmamma. "Or at least to something not directly poisonous."

"Hope for the best and prepare for the worst," little My observed with a chuckle.

They continued their work in peaceful silence.

77

Suddenly there were a few light taps on the glass pane in the door, and without waiting for an answer Too-ticky came in and shook the rain off her oilskin jacket. Then she held the door open and called out in the dark, "Well, come along!"

"Whom are you bringing?" Moomintroll asked.

"It's Ninny," Too-ticky said. "Yes, her name's Ninny."

She still held the door open, wait-ing. No one came.

"Oh, well," Too-ticky said and shrugged her shoul-ders. "If she's too shy she'd better stay there for a while."

"She'll be drenched through," said Moominmamma.

"Perhaps that won't matter much when one's invisi-ble," Too-ticky said and sat down by the table. The family stopped working and waited for an explanation.

"You all know, don't you, that if people are frightened very often, they sometimes become invisible," Too-ticky said and swallowed a small egg mushroom that looked like a little snowball. "Well. This Ninny was fright-ened the wrong way by a lady who had taken care of her without really liking her. I've met this lady, and she was horrid. Not the angry sort, you know, which would have been understandable. No, she was the icily ironical kind."

"What's ironical?" Moomintroll asked.

"Well, imagine that you slip on a rotten mushroom and sit down on the basket of newly picked ones," Too-ticky said. "The natural thing for your mother would be to be angry. But no, she isn't. Instead she says, very coldly, 'I understand that's your idea of a graceful dance, but I'd thank you not to do it in people's food.' Something like that."

"How unpleasant," Moomintroll said.

"Yes, isn't it," replied Too-ticky. "This was the way this lady used to talk. She was ironic all day long every day, and finally the kid started to turn pale and fade around the edges, and less and less was seen of her. Last Friday one couldn't catch sight of her at all. The lady gave her away to me and said she really couldn't take care of relatives she couldn't even see."

"And what did you do to the lady?" My asked with bulging eyes. "Did you bash her head?"

"That's of no use with the ironic sort," Too-ticky said. "I took Ninny home with me, of course. And now I've brought her here for you to make her visible again."

There was a slight pause. Only the rain was heard, rustling along over the veranda roof. Everybody stared at Too-ticky and thought for a while.

"Does she talk?" Moominpappa asked.

"No. But the lady has hung a small silver bell around her neck so that one can hear where she is."

Too-ticky arose and opened the door again. "Ninny!" she called out in the dark.

The cool smell of autumn crept in from the garden, and a square of light threw itself on the wet grass. After a while there was a slight tinkle outside, rather hesitantly. The sound came up the

steps and stopped. A bit above the floor a small silver bell was seen hanging in the air on a black ribbon. Ninny seemed to have a very thin neck.

"All right," Too-ticky said. "Now, here's your new family. They're a bit silly at times, but rather decent, largely speaking."

"Give the kid a chair," Moominpappa said. "Does she know how to pick mushrooms?"

"I really know nothing at all about Ninny," Too-ticky said. "I've only brought her here and told you what I know. Now I have a few other things to attend to. Please look in some day, won't you, and let me know how you get along. Cheerio."

When Too-ticky had gone the family sat quite silent, looking at the empty chair and the silver bell. After a while one of the chanterelles slowly rose from the heap on the table. Invisible paws picked it clean from needles and earth. Then it was cut to pieces, and the pieces drifted away and laid themselves in the basin. Another mushroom sailed up from the table.

"Thrilling!" My said with awe. "Try to give her something to eat. I'd like to know if you can see the food when she swallows it."

"How on earth does one make her visible again?" Moominpappa said worriedly. "Should we take her to a doctor?"

"I don't think so," said Moominmamma. "I believe she wants to be invisible for a while. Too-ticky said she's shy. Better leave the kid alone until something turns up."

And so it was decided.

The eastern attic room happened to be unoccupied, so Moominmamma made Ninny a bed there. The silver bell tinkled along after her upstairs and reminded Moominmamma of the cat that once had lived with them. At the bedside she laid out the apple, the glass of juice, and the three striped pieces of candy everybody in the house was given at bedtime.

Then she lighted a candle and said:

"Now have a good sleep, Ninny. Sleep as late as you can. There'll be tea for you in the morning any time you want. And if you happen to get a funny feeling or if you want anything, just come downstairs and tinkle."

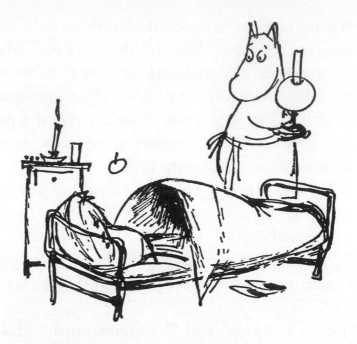

Moominmamma saw the quilt raise itself to form a very small mound. A dent appeared in the pillow. She went downstairs again to her own room and started looking through Granny's old notes about Infallible Household Remedies. Evil Eye. Melancholy. Colds. No. There didn't seem to be anything suitable. Yes, there was. Toward the end of the notebook she found a few lines written down at the time when Granny's hand was already rather shaky. "If people start getting misty and difficult to see." Good. Moominmamma read the recipe, which was rather complicated, and started at once to mix the medicine for little Ninny.

The bell came tinkling downstairs, one step at a time, with a small pause between each step. Moomintroll had waited for it all morning. But the silver bell wasn't the exciting thing. That was the paws. Ninny's paws were coming down the steps. They were very small, with anxiously bunched toes. Nothing else of Ninny was visible. It was very odd.

Moomintroll drew back behind the porcelain stove and stared bewitchedly at the paws that passed him on their way to the veranda. Now she served herself some tea. The cup was raised in the air and sank back again. She ate some bread and butter and marmalade. Then the cup and saucer drifted away to the kitchen, were washed and put away in the closet. You see, Ninny was a very orderly little child.

Moomintroll rushed out in the garden and shouted, "Mamma! She's got paws! You can see her paws!"

I thought as much, Moominmamma was thinking where she sat high in the apple tree. Granny knew a thing or two. Now when the medicine starts to work we'll be on the right way.

"Splendid," said Moominpappa. "And better still when she shows her snout one day. It makes me feel sad to talk with people who are invisible. And who never answer me."

"Hush, dear," Moominmamma said warningly. Ninny's paws were standing in the grass among the fallen apples.

"Hello Ninny," shouted My. "You've slept like a hog. When are you going to show your snout? You must look a fright if you've wanted to be invisible."

"Shut up," Moomintroll whispered, "she'll be hurt." He went running up to Ninny and said:

"Never mind My. She's hard-boiled. You're really safe here among us. Don't even think about that horrid lady. She can't come here and take you away. . . ."

In a moment Ninny's paws had faded away and become nearly indistinguishable from the grass.

"Darling, you're an ass," said Moominmamma. "You can't go about reminding the kid about those things. Now pick apples and don't talk rubbish."

They all picked apples.

After a while Ninny's paws became clearer again and climbed one of the trees.

It was a beautiful autumn morning. The shadows made one's snout a little chilly but the sunshine felt nearly like summer. Everything was wet from the night's rain, and all colors were strong and clear. When all the apples were picked or shaken down, Moominpappa carried the biggest apple mincer out in the garden, and they started making apple-cheese.

Moomintroll turned the handle, Moominmamma fed the mincer with apples, and Moominpappa carried the filled jars to the veranda. Little My sat in a tree singing the Big Apple Song.

Suddenly there was a crash.

On the garden path appeared a large heap of apple-cheese, all prickly with glass splinters. Beside the heap one could see Ninny's paws, rapidly fading away.

"Oh," said Moominmamma. "That was the jar we use to give to the bumblebees. Now we needn't carry it down to the field. And Granny always said that if you want the earth to grow something for you, then you have to give it a present in the autumn."

Ninny's paws appeared back again, and above them a pair of spindly legs came to view. Above the legs one could see the faint outline of a brown dress hem.

"I can see her legs!" cried Moomintroll.

"Congrats," said little My, looking down out of her tree. "Not bad. But the Groke knows why you must wear snuff-brown."

Moominmamma nodded to herself and sent a thought to her Granny and the medicine.

Ninny padded along after them all day. They became used to the tinkle and no longer thought Ninny very remarkable.

By evening they had nearly forgotten about her. But when everybody was in bed Moominmamma took out a rose-pink shawl of hers and made it into a little dress. When it was ready she carried it upstairs to the eastern attic room and cautiously laid it out on a chair. Then she made a broad hair ribbon out of the material left over.

Moominmamma was enjoying herself tremendously. It was exactly like sewing doll's clothes again. And the funny thing was that one didn't know if the doll had yellow or black hair.

The following day Ninny had her dress on. She was visible up to her neck, and when she came down to morning tea she bobbed and piped:

"Thank you all ever so much."

The family felt very embarrassed, and no one found anything to say. Also it was hard to know where to look when one talked to Ninny. Of course one tried to look a bit above the bell where Ninny was supposed to have her eyes. But then very easily one found oneself staring at some of the visible things further down instead, and it gave one an impolite feeling.

Moominpappa cleared his throat. "We're happy to see," he started, "that we see more of Ninny today. The more we see the happier we are. . . ."

My gave a laugh and banged the table with her spoon. "Fine that you've started talking," she said. "Hope you have anything to say. Do you know any good games?"

"No," Ninny piped. "But I've heard about games."

Moomintroll was delighted. He decided to teach Ninny all the games he knew.

After coffee all three of them went down to the river to play. Only Ninny turned out to be quite impossible. She bobbed and nodded and very seriously replied, quite, and how funny, and of course, but it was clear to all that she played only from politeness and not to have fun.

"Run, run, can't you!" My cried. "Or can't you even jump?"

Ninny's thin legs duti-fully ran and jumped. Then she stood still again with arms dangling. The empty dress neck over the bell was looking strangely helpless.

"D'you think anybody likes that?" My cried. "Haven't you any life in you? D'you want a biff on the nose?"

"Rather not," Ninny piped humbly.

"She can't play," mumbled Moomintroll.

"She can't get angry," little My said. "That's what's wrong with her. Listen, you," My continued and went close to Ninny with a menacing look. "You'll never have a face of your own until you've learned to fight. Believe me."

87

"Yes, of course," Ninny replied, cautiously backing away.

There was no further turn for the better.

At last they stopped trying to teach Ninny to play. She didn't like funny stories either. She never laughed at the right places. She never laughed at all, in fact. This had a depressing effect on the person who told the story. And she was left alone to herself.

Days went by, and Ninny was still without a face. They became accustomed to seeing her pink dress marching along behind Moominmamma. As soon as Moominmamma stopped, the silver bell also stopped, and when she continued her way the bell began tinkling again. A bit above the dress a big rose-pink bow was bobbing in thin air.

Moominmamma continued to treat Ninny with Granny's medicine, but nothing further happened. So after some time she stopped the treatment, thinking that many people had managed all right before without a head, and besides perhaps Ninny wasn't very good-looking.

Now everyone could imagine for himself what she looked like, and this can often brighten up a relationship.

One day the family went off through the wood down to the beach. They were going to pull the boat up for winter. Ninny came tinkling behind as usual, but when they came in view of the sea she suddenly stopped. Then she lay down on her stomach in the sand and started to whine.

"What's come over Ninny? Is she frightened?" asked Moominpappa.

"Perhaps she hasn't seen the sea before," Moominmamma said. She stooped and exchanged a few whispering words with Ninny. Then she straightened up again and said:

"No, it's the first time. Ninny thinks the sea's too big."

"Of all the silly kids," little My started, but Moominmamma gave her a severe look and said, "Don't be a silly kid yourself. Now let's pull the boat ashore."

They went out on the landing stage to the bathing hut where Too-ticky lived, and knocked at the door.

"Hullo," Too-ticky said, "how's the invisible child?"

"There's only her snout left," Moominpappa replied. "At the moment she's a bit startled but it'll pass over. Can you lend us a hand with the boat?"

"Certainly," Too-ticky said.

While the boat was pulled ashore and turned keel upward Ninny had padded down to the water's edge and was standing immobile on the wet sand. They left her alone.

Moominmamma sat down on the landing stage and looked down into the water. "Dear me, how cold it looks," she said. And then she yawned a bit and added that nothing exciting had happened for weeks.

Moominpappa gave Moomintroll a wink, pulled a horrible face, and started to steal up to Moominmamma from behind.

Of course, he didn't really think of pushing her in the water as he had done many times when she was young. Perhaps he didn't even want to startle her, but just to amuse the kids a little.

But before he reached her a sharp cry was heard, a pink streak of lightning shot over the landing stage, and Moominpappa let out a scream and dropped his hat into the water. Ninny had sunk her small invisible teeth in Moominpappa's tail, and they were sharp.

"Good work!" cried My. "I couldn't have done it better myself!"

Ninny was standing on the landing stage. She had a small, snub-nosed, angry face below a red tangle of hair. She was hissing at Moominpappa like a cat.

"Don't you *dare* push her into the big horrible sea!" she cried.

"I see her, I see her!" shouted Moomintroll. "She's sweet!"

"Sweet my eye," said Moominpappa, inspecting his bitten tail. "She's the silliest, nastiest, badly-brought-uppest child I've ever seen, with or without a head."

He knelt down on the landing stage and tried to fish for his hat with a stick. And in some mysterious way he managed to tip himself over, and tumbled in on his head.

90

He came up at once, standing safely on the bottom, with his snout above water and his ears filled with mud.

"Oh dear!" Ninny was shouting. "Oh, how great! Oh, how funny!"

The landing stage shook with her laughter.

"I believe she's never laughed before," Too-ticky said wonderingly. "You seem to have changed her; she's even worse than little My. But the main thing is that one can see her, of course."

"It's all thanks to Granny," Moominmamma said.

Theme Introduction

Fitting In

In this section of the book, you will read about characters who have trouble fitting in with others. Thinking about these stories, and about your own experiences fitting in, will give you new ideas about what it means to fit in.

Important Questions to Think About

Before starting this section, think about your own experiences fitting in:

- Have you ever felt as though you didn't belong somewhere?
- Do you change how you act when you're around different people?

Once you have thought about your own experiences with fitting in, think about this **theme question** and write down your answers or share them aloud:

What makes it hard or easy for someone to fit in?

After reading each story in this section, ask yourself the theme question again. You may have some new ideas you want to add.

It was the best day of my life.

THE COMING
OF THE SURFMAN

Peter Collington

There are two gangs in my neighborhood: the Hammers and the Nails. They are sworn enemies.

I was skateboarding home one day when the Hammer gang grabbed me. Their leader, Hammerhead, lifted me off the ground by my collar, pushed his face close to mine, and showed me his fist. "You're joining us," he said. It wasn't an invitation. It was a statement of fact. As I might want to smile again sometime—and it would be essential I had some teeth to do it with—I nodded.

"A wise decision," Hammerhead said, putting me down. "Now wear this." He handed me a red bandanna, the Hammers' color. As I walked away, struggling to put it around my head, I noticed the Nail gang up ahead. I quickly stuffed the bandanna into my pocket.

Nailhead, the gang leader, looked me over. My foot tapped nervously on my skateboard. Nailhead's eyes lowered to my board.

"You wanna grow up. Skateboards are for kids." As I *was* a kid, it was quite logical that I should have a skateboard, but something made me keep quiet. It was my teeth again. Nailhead handed me a blue bandanna. "Wear this," he said. "You're one of us."

So I belong to two gangs, and if either of them finds out, I'm done for.

That night, I was lying awake thinking about my predicament when I heard a motor running. I looked out of my bedroom window and saw a van parked opposite, outside the boarded-up store. A man wearing beachwear stepped out. He looked around, the streetlight flashing on his sunglasses, and walked over to the store's front door. He jiggled with some keys and went in. He began unloading long cardboard cartons from his van.

After a while, I must have dropped off to sleep, but I was woken by the sound of an electric sander moaning and whining. The man had taken down the boards from the store window and was now working on the peeling paint.

The old store had closed down long ago because the owner was fed up with vandals breaking his windows and with neighborhood gangs harassing his customers. So a new store would be welcome.

The man had now opened some paint cans and was brightening up the woodwork. I couldn't wait until morning to find out what kind of a store it was going to be. A pizza place, a video rental shop—even a new food store would be fine. We wouldn't have to lug groceries from eight blocks away anymore.

Then my heart sank. I remembered the gangs and what they might do to me tomorrow.

When I got up and went outside, the two gangs were waiting for me. At least that's what I thought at first, but then I noticed they weren't looking at me but at the new store. The gangs stood well apart and were pointing to the window display. Both Hammerhead and Nailhead took turns laughing and their respective gangs imitated them. The name of the store, emblazoned in bright neon lights, was SURFING SUPPLIES. In the store window were surfboards and different types of surfing wear.

I began to laugh myself, partly out of relief that the gangs had forgotten about me and partly because I shared their amusement. It was quite simple. There was

nowhere around here to surf. The beach was a two-day drive away.

Who would open a store selling surfing stuff in a run-down neighborhood like this? Only someone who was two bread rolls short of a picnic. Someone who was seriously weird. The gangs laughed, and I laughed with them.

The SURFING SUPPLIES store opened regularly at nine o'clock every morning and closed at five thirty on the dot. No one went into the store to buy anything, and no one came out.

The store owner became known as the Surfman, and people hooted and laughed whenever his name was mentioned. I didn't know what to think, but I was glad about one thing. Since he had come, the Hammers and Nails had forgotten entirely about me and hardly fought each other anymore. The blank, angry stares were gone; expression was leaking into their faces. I had seen that look before—especially in cats. It was a look of obsessive curiosity. Their brains were straining to figure out why the Surfman was here. Anyone weird could also be dangerous. So both gangs set up around-the-clock surveillance.

A pattern of behavior was emerging. Every Monday morning the Surfman cleaned his windows and swept the sidewalk. Once a month he took stock, even though he had sold nothing. High-intensity binoculars revealed that he ate a mixed salad and yogurt for lunch and ran 200 miles a week on his exercise machine. He *had* to be training for something—but what?

Then one night I spotted him. He came out of his store about eleven o'clock and walked over to the abandoned factory across the way. He took out a large piece of paper and studied it by flashlight. He looked up at the factory and then down at the sheet of paper. He walked around the factory for a while and then went back to the store.

After this, the Surfman started appearing regularly at night, carrying a toolkit. He had more in common with the gangs than I had at first thought: he was very good at wrecking things. He was systematically demolishing the factory. It was crazy. Each night there was hammering and banging for hours on end. But as the weeks went by, there seemed to be some method in his madness.

With the help of the old factory crane, the Surfman ripped off the factory roof and sent the metal sheets crashing down onto the floor below. Then he began bolting the sheets onto the inner walls and floor. His long shadow spilled out over the ground as the light from

his welding equipment flickered and
darted. The Surfman rolled large pipes
from the back of the factory and collected them together by the pump.
Then he started bolting them together.

At the end of his night shift, he
would stagger home, tired and drained,
but he always opened the store, regular
as clockwork, at nine o'clock, even
though no one had ever seen a cus-
tomer go in.

I began to really feel for him. He
reminded me of my late dad, always
working hard and no one giving him
any thanks.

One evening, the Surfman erected
scaffolding in front of the two giant
storages tanks and, with cutting equipment, began burning into the metal.
Every night something new was added
or changed, and in the light of day
the two gangs would check out the
Surfman's progress. Occasionally, the
gangs would take turns flexing their
muscles and knocking something
down. But their hearts weren't really
in it, and when the Surfman repaired
the damage, they just shrugged and let
things stand.

They, like me, wanted to see the Surfman complete his work. We were all enthralled. We were trembling with anticipation. We all knew what the Surfman was building, but nobody put it into words. The Surfman jokes had died away, and a certain grudging respect was apparent. He might be a weird guy, but he was a weird guy who was making something for us. Something we had wanted all our lives.

One night, I was woken by the sound of running water. The Surfman was standing by the metal pipes turning a large wheel tap. He was wearing swimwear. As he pressed a switch, the pump started throbbing and vibrating. The Surfman picked up his surfboard and climbed high up the metal ladder to a position overlooking the empty factory below. He leaned forward and pulled a lever. The doors of the two storage tanks sprang open, and WATER gushed out with all the ferocity of a giant surfing wave! The Surfman was swept from his perch, only to reappear with his surfboard under his feet and his arms stretched out on either side. *The Surfman was surfing!* He rode the wave all the way to the end of the factory, was carried up the metal slope, and then plummeted ski-slope-style onto the piled-up car tires below.

The Surfman retrieved his surfboard and clambered down the tires. With his surfboard under his arm, he walked over to his store and went in. The wave machine wheezed and coughed, then spluttered to a halt. I always knew what it was going to be, but now I screamed the

words out loud: "It's a WAVE MACHINE!" My voice echoed out of the window and ricocheted around the neighborhood. I heard whoops and cries of joy from Hammerhead and Nailhead, who had witnessed it too.

Tomorrow was going to be a great day.

In the morning, the two gangs were there early, clutching bits of wood and anything else they thought might do for a surfboard. When the wave machine started up, the gangs clambered up the ladder and, mixing together like one happy family, launched themselves and their bits of wood onto the wave. I just stood and watched. This was going to be fun. None of them had the slightest idea of how to surf, so they sank with their bits of wood and came up with furious faces, spurting water.

I had been saving up money for some time, not quite sure what to do with it. Now I *knew*! As my dad used to say, "To do the job right, you need the right tool."

I walked over to the SURFING SUPPLIES store and put down my money. The Surfman handed me a real beauty of a board. He wasn't a talkative sort of guy. But as I left, he turned and said, "Have a good day."

I walked over to the wave machine and climbed up the stairs. The gangs stood back to watch. I waited until I heard the crash of water, and as the wave came, I stepped off. All that skateboarding had been good training. I held my balance and rode the crest of the wave for all it was worth. It was the best day of my life. The gangs tried to follow my example, but they had no balance, and their boards were rubbish. They knew what they had to do.

Nailhead led his gang in first. They all bought surfboards and walked proudly out of the Surfman's store. Next, Hammerhead led his gang into the store. When the Hammers came out, Nailhead was there to confront them. He swallowed hard. The words did not come easy to him.

"You wanna have a truce?" he asked.

Hammerhead looked back at his gang. They all nodded their heads. "Okay," said Hammerhead. "We surf alternate days." He held out his hand to shake.

"Done," said Nailhead.

The two gangs beamed at each other.

Nailhead took out a coin. "Heads or tails?"

Nailhead and his gang won the toss, and cheering, they ran over to the wave machine to try out their boards.

I put on my blue bandanna and joined them. The next day, I put on my red bandanna and joined the Hammers.

After a week, they found me out. I was thrown out of both gangs, and my surfing days were over. All I could do now was watch. I felt bored and depressed. Without surfing, life felt almost not worth living.

One day, I was enviously watching one of the gangs surfing when the pump suddenly ground to a halt. A cry of pain went up from every gang member's throat. The wave machine had broken down.

That evening, the Surfman came out of his shop and called me over. He handed me his toolkit, and I walked behind him over to the wave machine. I handed him each tool as he requested it, and when the job was finished, he turned to me and said, "Okay, try it out." I ran home and got my surfboard. I couldn't believe my luck. I tried one wave, curling down its crest and zigzagging in front of it.

"How is it?" called the Surfman.

"Almost right," I answered. "I'll just check it out again." And this way I got to surf a second time—a long time— until I felt I was stretching the Surfman's patience and finally called out, "Yeah, it's fine now!" And the Surfman closed it down until the next day.

Fortunately, the wave machine broke down quite regularly, and I was always on hand to carry the Surfman's toolkit. As he worked, he talked to me, explaining what he was doing and why. He named each tool I handed to him as if he wanted me to remember what it was for the next time. The Surfman really did remind me of my late dad: *he* always

liked to have me stand by him when he was fixing things. But I did the same thing now that I used to do with my dad. I humored him. I nodded and said "Yeah" a few times as if I were paying attention. But my mind wasn't there. It was focused on surfing and silently crying out for that moment when the Surfman would turn to me and say, "Okay, it's fixed. Go try it out." Then life for me would begin. Floating on those short-lived waves was everything to me.

On their enforced day of rest, while one gang surfed, the other spent its time jogging to the health food store in the next neighborhood for more supplies or sitting around watching surfing movies they had rented from the Surfman's store, analyzing and discussing good moves.

Then the truce broke down. The wave machine had been out of action for a whole day, so the Hammers felt they should surf the next day. The Nails insisted it was their turn, and fighting broke out. The Hammers, anticipating trouble, had come prepared. They had hidden their

own surfboards, and producing axes and sledgehammers, they rushed over to the Nails' surfboards and began smashing them.

The result was catastrophic. The Nails let out agonizing screams of pain and doubled over on the ground, hugging the remains of their surfboards. They clutched them like babies and went home brokenhearted to try and fix them. The Hammers felt powerful—they had never been happier. They surfed all that day, confident that they would be surfing every day from now on.

But somehow I knew that would not be the end of it.

That night, I was woken by the sound of banging and crashing. Looking out of my bedroom window, I saw the Nail gang wielding axes and sledgehammers. They were smashing the wave machine. I quickly dressed and ran out to try and stop them. But it was too late. The Hammer gang was there too, and a big battle was taking place. I shouted and tried to reason with them, but no one took any notice of me. Water was spurting out of the pipes, and sparks were flying everywhere.

The following day, the two battle-weary and dejected gangs stood in front of the wave machine and looked at the damage they had caused. Their eyes looked over toward the Surfman's store. He had fixed things before. Surely he would fix things again.

Later that evening, I watched the Surfman walk out of his store and across to the battered wave machine. He stood for some time, just shaking his head. Then he walked home and into his store.

The next morning the Surfman had gone. His store was empty and the wave machine unrepaired. The two gangs stood in silence. Big tears rolled down their faces.

I ran back home to get my late dad's toolkit. The two gangs stepped aside to let me work. I tried various tools, pulling this way and that. But I knew in my heart it was hopeless. I couldn't remember what the Surfman had told me. I hadn't been listening. The gangs' hopeful eyes narrowed.

"Stupid kid," they said, and walked away.

Things have gone pretty much back to normal here, the gangs once again fighting each other. Neither of them is interested in my joining them now, which is fine by me.

On bad days, I think about my father a lot and all the things I could have done with him if he were still alive. On good days, I feel sure that the Surfman will return, and this time I know I'll be ready and really listen to what he says and really watch his big hands as he works away at the rusting hulk of the wave machine, restoring it to good working order.

The jungle burned with sunlight.

ALL SUMMER IN A DAY

Ray Bradbury

R eady?"

"Ready."

"Now?"

"Soon."

"Do the scientists really know? Will it happen today, will it?"

"Look, look; see for yourself!"

The children pressed to each other like so many roses, so many weeds, intermixed, peering out for a look at the hidden sun.

It rained.

It had been raining for seven years; thousands upon thousands of days compounded and filled from one end to the other with rain, with the drum and gush of water, with the sweet crystal fall of showers and the concussion of storms so heavy they were tidal waves come over the islands. A thousand forests had been crushed under the rain and grown up a thousand times to be crushed again. And this was the way life was forever on the planet Venus, and this was the schoolroom of the children of the rocket men and women who had come to a raining world to set up civilization and live out their lives.

"It's stopping, it's stopping!"

"Yes, yes!"

Margot stood apart from them, from these children who could never remember a time when there wasn't rain and rain and rain. They were all nine years old, and if there had been a day, seven years ago, when the sun came out for an hour and showed its face to the stunned world, they could not recall. Sometimes, at night, she heard them stir, in remembrance, and she knew they were dreaming and remembering gold or a yellow crayon or a coin large enough to buy the world with. She knew they thought they remembered a warmness, like a blushing in the face, in the body, in the arms and legs and trembling hands. But then they always awoke to the tatting drum, the endless shaking down of clear bead necklaces upon the roof, the walk, the gardens, the forests, and their dreams were gone.

All day yesterday they had read in class about the sun. About how like a lemon it was, and how hot. And they had written small stories or essays or poems about it:

I think the sun is a flower,
That blooms for just one hour.

That was Margot's poem, read in a quiet voice in the still classroom while the rain was falling outside.

"Aw, you didn't write that!" protested one of the boys.

"I did," said Margot. "I *did*."

"William!" said the teacher.

But that was yesterday. Now the rain was slackening, and the children were crushed in the great thick windows.

"Where's teacher?"

"She'll be back."

"She'd better hurry; we'll miss it!"

They turned on themselves, like a feverish wheel, all tumbling spokes.

Margot stood alone. She was a very frail girl who looked as if she had been lost in the rain for years and the rain had washed out the blue from her eyes and the red from her mouth and the yellow from her hair. She was an old photograph dusted from an album, whitened away, and if she spoke at all her voice would be a ghost. Now she stood, separate, staring at the rain and the loud wet world beyond the huge glass.

"What're *you* looking at?" said William.

Margot said nothing.

111

"Speak when you're spoken to." He gave her a shove. But she did not move; rather she let herself be moved only by him and nothing else.

They edged away from her; they would not look at her. She felt them go away. And this was because she would play no games with them in the echoing tunnels of the underground city. If they tagged her and ran, she stood blinking after them and did not follow. When the class sang songs about happiness and life and games, her lips barely moved. Only when they sang about the sun and the summer did her lips move as she watched the drenched windows.

And then, of course, the biggest crime of all was that she had come here only five years ago from Earth, and she remembered the sun and the way the sun was and the sky was when she was four in Ohio. And they, they had been on Venus all their lives, and they had been only two years old when last the sun came out and had long since forgotten the color and heat of it and the way it really was. But Margot remembered.

"It's like a penny," she said once, eyes closed.

"No, it's not!" the children cried.

"It's like a fire," she said, "in the stove."

"You're lying, you don't remember!" cried the children.

But she remembered and stood quietly apart from all of them and watched the patterning windows. And once, a month ago, she had refused to shower in the school shower rooms, had clutched her hands to her ears and over her head, screaming the water mustn't touch her head. So after that, dimly, dimly, she sensed it, she was different, and they knew her difference and kept away.

There was talk that her father and mother were taking her back to Earth next year; it seemed vital to her that they do so, though it would mean the loss of thousands of dollars to her family. And so, the children hated her for all these reasons of big and little consequence. They hated her pale snow face, her waiting silence, her thinness, and her possible future.

"Get away!" The boy gave her another push. "What're you waiting for?"

Then, for the first time, she turned and looked at him. And what she was waiting for was in her eyes.

"Well, don't wait around here!" cried the boy savagely. "You won't see nothing!"

Her lips moved.

"Nothing!" he cried. "It was all a joke, wasn't it?" He turned to the other children. "Nothing's happening today. *Is* it?"

They all blinked at him and then, understanding, laughed and shook their heads. "Nothing, nothing!"

"Oh, but," Margot whispered, her eyes helpless. "But this is the day, the scientists predict, they say, they *know*, the sun . . . "

"All a joke!" said the boy, and seized her roughly. "Hey, everyone, let's put her in a closet before teacher comes!"

"No," said Margot, falling back.

They surged about her, caught her up, and bore her, protesting, and then pleading, and then crying, back into a tunnel, a room, a closet, where they slammed and locked the door. They stood looking at the door and saw it tremble from her beating and throwing herself against it. They heard her muffled cries. Then, smiling, they turned and went out and back down the tunnel, just as the teacher arrived.

"Ready, children?" She glanced at her watch.

"Yes!" said everyone.

"Are we all here?"

"Yes!"

The rain slackened still more.

They crowded to the huge door.

The rain stopped.

It was as if, in the midst of a film concerning an avalanche, a tornado, a hurricane, a volcanic eruption, something had, first, gone wrong with the sound apparatus, thus muffling and finally cutting off all noise, all of the blasts and repercussions and thunders, and then, second, ripped the film from the projector and inserted in its place a peaceful tropical slide which did not move or tremor. The world ground to a standstill. The silence was so immense and unbelievable that you felt your ears had been stuffed or you had lost your hearing altogether. The children put their hands to their ears. They stood apart. The door slid back, and the smell of the silent, waiting world came in to them.

The sun came out.

It was the color of flaming bronze, and it was very large. And the sky around it was a blazing blue tile color. And the jungle burned with sunlight as the children, released from their spell, rushed out, yelling, into the springtime.

"Now, don't go too far," called the teacher after them. "You've only two hours, you know. You wouldn't want to get caught out!"

But they were running and turning their faces up to the sky and feeling the sun on their cheeks like a warm iron; they were taking off their jackets and letting the sun burn their arms.

"Oh, it's better than the sun lamps, isn't it?"

"Much, much better!"

They stopped running and stood in the great jungle that covered Venus, that grew and never stopped growing, tumultuously, even as you watched it. It was a nest of octopi, clustering up great arms of fleshlike weed, wavering, flowering in this brief spring. It was the color of rubber and ash, this jungle, from the many years without sun. It was the color of stones and white cheeses and ink, and it was the color of the moon.

The children lay out, laughing, on the jungle mattress, and heard it sigh and squeak under them, resilient and alive. They ran among the trees, they slipped and fell, they pushed each other, they played hide-and-seek and tag, but most of all they squinted at the sun until tears ran down their faces, they put their hands up to that yellowness and that amazing blueness, and they breathed of the fresh, fresh air and listened and listened to the silence which suspended them in a blessed sea of no sound and no motion. They looked at everything and savored everything. Then, wildly, like animals escaped from their caves, they ran and ran in shouting circles. They ran for an hour and did not stop running.

And then—

In the midst of their running one of the girls wailed.

Everyone stopped.

The girl, standing in the open, held out her hand.

"Oh, look, look," she said, trembling.

They came slowly to look at her opened palm.

In the center of it, cupped and huge, was a single raindrop.

She began to cry, looking at it.

They glanced quietly at the sky.

"Oh. Oh."

A few cold drops fell on their noses and their cheeks and their mouths. The sun faded behind a stir of mist. A wind blew cool around them. They turned and started to walk back toward the underground house, their hands at their sides, their smiles vanishing away.

A boom of thunder startled them and, like leaves before a new hurricane, they tumbled upon each other and ran. Lightning struck ten miles away, five miles away, a mile, a half mile. The sky darkened into midnight in a flash.

They stood in the doorway of the underground for a moment until it was raining hard. Then they closed the door and heard the gigantic sound of the rain falling in tons and avalanches, everywhere and forever.

"Will it be seven more years?"

"Yes. Seven."

Then one of them gave a little cry.

"Margot!"

"What?"

"She's still in the closet where we locked her."

"Margot."

They stood as if someone had driven them, like so many stakes, into the floor. They looked at each other and then looked away. They glanced out at the world that was raining now and raining and raining steadily. They could not meet each other's glances. Their faces were solemn and pale. They looked at their hands and feet, their faces down.

"Margot."

One of the girls said, "Well . . . ?"

No one moved.

"Go on," whispered the girl.

They walked slowly down the hall in the sound of cold rain. They turned through the doorway to the room in the sound of the storm and thunder, lightning on their faces, blue and terrible. They walked over to the closet door slowly and stood by it.

Behind the closet door was only silence.

They unlocked the door, even more slowly, and let Margot out.

"Let's quit for a minute," Glennie suggested.

A GAME OF CATCH

Richard Wilbur

Monk and Glennie were playing catch on the side lawn of the firehouse when Scho caught sight of them. They were good at it, for seventh graders, as anyone could see right away. Monk, wearing a catcher's mitt, would lean easily sidewise and back, with one leg lifted and his throwing hand almost down to the grass, and then lob the white ball straight up into the sunlight. Glennie would shield his eyes with his left hand and, just as the ball fell past him, snag it with a little dart of his glove. Then he would burn the ball straight toward Monk, and it would spank into the round mitt and sit, like a still-life apple on a plate, until Monk flipped it over into his right hand and, with a negligent flick of his hanging arm, gave Glennie a fast grounder.

They were going on and on like that, in a kind of slow, mannered, luxurious dance in the sun, their faces perfectly blank and entranced, when Glennie noticed Scho dawdling along the other side of the street and called hello to him. Scho crossed over and stood at the front edge of the lawn, near an apple tree, watching.

"Got your glove?" asked Glennie after a time. Scho obviously hadn't.

"You could give me some easy grounders," said Scho. "But don't burn 'em."

"All right," Glennie said. He moved off a little, so the three of them formed a triangle, and they passed the ball around for about five minutes, Monk tossing easy grounders to Scho, Scho throwing to Glennie, and Glennie burning them in to Monk. After a while, Monk began to throw them back to Glennie once or twice before he let Scho have his grounder, and finally Monk gave Scho a fast, bumpy grounder that hopped over his shoulder and went into the brake on the other side of the street.

"Not so hard," called Scho as he ran across to get it.

"You should've had it," Monk shouted.

It took Scho a little while to find the ball among the ferns and dead leaves, and when he saw it, he grabbed it up and threw it toward Glennie. It struck the trunk of the apple tree, bounced back at an angle, and rolled steadily and stupidly onto the cement apron in front of the firehouse, where one of the trucks was parked. Scho ran hard and stopped it just before it rolled under the truck, and this time he carried it back to his former position on the lawn and threw it carefully to Glennie.

"I got an idea," said Glennie. "Why don't Monk and I catch for five minutes more, and then you can borrow one of our gloves?"

"That's all right with me," said Monk. He socked his fist into his mitt, and Glennie burned one in.

"All right," Scho said, and went over and sat under the tree. There in the shade he watched them resume their skillful play. They threw lazily fast or lazily slow—high, low, or wide—and always handsomely, their expressions serene, changeless, and forgetful. When Monk missed a low backhand catch, he walked indolently after the ball and, hardly even looking, flung it sidearm for an imaginary putout. After a good while of this, Scho said, "Isn't it five minutes yet?"

"One minute to go," said Monk, with a fraction of a grin.

Scho stood up and watched the ball slap back and forth for several minutes more, and then he turned and pulled himself up into the crotch of the tree.

"Where are you going?" Monk asked.

"Just up the tree," Scho said.

"I guess he doesn't want to catch," said Monk.

Scho went up and up through the fat light-gray branches until they grew slender and bright and gave under him. He found a place where several supple branches were knit to make a dangerous chair, and sat there with his head coming out of the leaves into the sunlight. He could see the two other boys down below, the ball going back and forth between them as if they were bowling on the grass, and Glennie's crew-cut head looking like a sea urchin.

"I found a wonderful seat up here," Scho said loudly. "If I don't fall out." Monk and Glennie didn't look up or comment, and so he began jouncing gently in his chair of branches and singing "Yo-ho, heave ho" in an exaggerated way.

"Do you know what, Monk?" he announced in a few moments. "I can make you two guys do anything I want. Catch that ball, Monk! Now you catch it, Glennie!"

"I was going to catch it anyway," Monk suddenly said. "You're not making anybody do anything when they're already going to do it anyway."

"I made you say what you just said," Scho replied joyfully.

"No, you didn't," said Monk, still throwing and catching but now less serenely absorbed in the game.

"That's what I wanted you to say," Scho said.

The ball bounded off the rim of Monk's mitt and plowed into a gladiolus bed beside the firehouse, and Monk ran to get it while Scho jounced in his treetop and sang, "I wanted you to miss that. Anything you do is what I wanted you to do."

"Let's quit for a minute," Glennie suggested.

"We might as well, until the peanut gallery shuts up," Monk said.

They went over and sat cross-legged in the shade of the tree. Scho looked down between his legs and saw them on the dim, spotty ground, saying nothing to one another. Glennie soon began abstractedly spinning his glove between his palms; Monk pulled his nose and stared out across the lawn.

"I want you to mess around with your nose, Monk," said Scho, giggling. Monk withdrew his hand from his face.

"Do that with your glove, Glennie," Scho persisted. "Monk, I want you to pull up hunks of grass and chew on it."

Glennie looked up and saw a self-delighted, intense face staring down at him through the leaves. "Stop being a dope and come down and we'll catch for a few minutes," he said.

Scho hesitated, and then said, in a tentatively mocking voice, "That's what I wanted you to say."

"All right, then, nuts to you," said Glennie.

"Why don't you keep quiet and stop bothering people?" Monk asked.

"I made you say that," Scho replied, softly.

"Shut up," Monk said.

"I made you say that, and I want you to be standing there looking sore. And I want you to climb up the tree. I'm making you do it!"

Monk was scrambling up through the branches, awkward in his haste, and getting snagged on twigs. His face was furious and foolish, and he kept telling Scho to shut up, shut up, shut up, while the other's exuberant and panicky voice poured down upon his head.

"Now you shut up or you'll be sorry," Monk said, breathing hard as he reached up and threatened to shake the cradle of slight branches in which Scho was sitting.

"I *want*—" Scho screamed as he fell. Two lower branches broke his rustling, crackling fall, but he landed on his back with a deep thud and lay still, with a strangled look on his face and his eyes clenched. Glennie knelt down and asked breathlessly, "Are you OK, Scho? Are you OK?" while Monk swung down through the leaves crying that honestly he hadn't even touched him, the crazy guy just let go. Scho doubled up and turned over on his right side, and now both the other boys knelt beside him, pawing at his shoulder and begging to know how he was.

Then Scho rolled away from them and sat partly up, still struggling to get his wind but forcing a species of smile onto his face.

"I'm sorry, Scho," Monk said. "I didn't mean to make you fall."

Scho's voice came out weak and gravelly, in gasps. "I meant—you to do it. You—had to. You can't do—anything—unless I want—you to."

Glennie and Monk looked helplessly at him as he sat there, breathing a bit more easily and smiling fixedly, with tears in his eyes. Then they picked up their gloves and the ball, walked over to the street, and went slowly away down the sidewalk, Monk punching his fist into the mitt, Glennie juggling the ball between glove and hand.

From under the apple tree, Scho, still bent over a little for lack of breath, croaked after them in triumph and misery, "I want you to do whatever you're going to do for the whole rest of your life!"

A Guide to Question Types

Below are different types of questions you might ask while reading. Notice that it isn't always important (or even possible) to answer all questions right away. The questions below are about "Charles" (pp. 13–21).

Factual questions are about the story and have one correct answer that you can find by looking back at the story.

> **What grade is Laurie in?**
> (Answer: Kindergarten.)
>
> **Why does Laurie's mother miss the first Parent-Teachers meeting?**
> (Answer: The baby has a cold.)

Vocabulary questions are about words or phrases in the story. They can be answered with the glossary (pp. 131–151), a dictionary, or *context clues*—parts of the story near the word that give hints about its meaning.

> **What does "incredulously" mean?**
>
> **What is a "reformation"?**
> (Practice finding context clues on p. 18 to figure out the meaning of this word.)

Background questions are often about a story's location, time period, or culture. You can answer them with information from a source like the Internet or an encyclopedia.

> **When were teachers allowed to spank students?**
>
> **What happens at a PTA meeting?**

Speculative questions ask about events or details that are not covered in the story. You must guess at or invent your answers.

> What does Laurie's father do for a living?
>
> Will Laurie grow up to be a writer?

Evaluative questions ask for your personal opinion about something in the story, like whether a character does the right thing. These questions have more than one good answer. Support for these answers comes from your beliefs and experiences as well as the story.

> Are Laurie's parents strict enough with him when he is rude and misbehaves?
>
> Would you want to be friends with someone like Laurie?

Interpretive questions ask about the deep meaning of the story and are the focus of a Shared Inquiry discussion. They have more than one good answer. Support for these answers comes only from evidence in the story.

> Why doesn't Laurie wave goodbye to his mother when he leaves for the first day of school?
>
> Why are Laurie's parents so interested in his stories about Charles?

GLOSSARY

In this glossary, you'll find definitions for words that you may not know but that are in the stories you've read. You'll find the meaning of each word as it is used in the story. The word may have other meanings as well, which you can find in a dictionary if you're interested. If you don't find a word here that you are wondering about, go to your dictionary for help.

abstractedly: When you do something **abstractedly**, you do it while lost in thought. *The boy stared **abstractedly** out the window, paying no attention to his friends.*

accustomed: If you are **accustomed** to something, you are used to it. *If you are on a sports team, you grow **accustomed** to having after-school practice every week.*

anticipating: When you **anticipate** something, you think about it and prepare for it before it happens. ***Anticipating** the first day of summer vacation, we made plans to swim, bike, and camp.*

apparatus: The thing or things used for a certain job or purpose. *A magnet, a dish of water, and a pin are the **apparatus** you need to make a simple compass.*

avalanche: An **avalanche** is a large amount of earth, ice, or snow that falls suddenly down a mountainside. *Several mountain climbers were injured by the* **avalanche**.

awed: To be **awed** is to feel a mixture of wonder, respect, and a little fear. *The audience was* **awed** *when the magician pulled a rabbit out of a hat.*

barrack: A building where soldiers or workers and their families live.

bazaar: A market with many booths or small shops.

beckoned: When you **beckon**, you say or do something that shows you want someone or something to come closer. *My mother* **beckoned** *me to her side by waving her hand.*

bewitchedly: If you behave **bewitchedly**, you act so interested it seems as if you are under a spell. *The children gazed* **bewitchedly** *at the fireflies glowing in the dark.*

biff: A hit or a punch. *My sister gave me a* **biff** *on the shoulder when I made fun of her.*

bluff: A steep, tall cliff or bank. *The climbers went to the top of the* **bluff** *so they could look down at the ocean.*

bracero: A Spanish word for a farm worker from Mexico who works in the United States for short periods of time.

brake: An area where bushes and trees have grown very thickly.

bungled: To **bungle** something is to do it badly or clumsily. *The sink is leaking again because the plumber **bungled** the job.*

burden: Something heavy to carry. *The student was happy to set down the **burden** of his overstuffed backpack.* A **burden** is also a serious responsibility that is often hard to deal with. *Lifeguards have the **burden** of saving people from drowning.*

capable: Having the power or skill to do something. *A strong person is more **capable** of lifting heavy loads than a weak person.*

catastrophic: Causing great damage or ruin, often very suddenly. *The **catastrophic** oil spill killed thousands of animals and birds.*

chanterelles: Edible mushrooms that are orange or yellow and trumpet shaped.

cheerio: A friendly way of saying "goodbye!" or "see you later!"

civilization: The culture and ways of life that develop within a certain group or area of the world. *The team of scientists studied the **civilization** of the ancient Romans.* **Civilization** also means a modern way of living. *After camping in the woods, you might be glad to return to **civilization**.*

clambered: To **clamber** is to climb with difficulty, often using both hands and feet. *The children **clambered** up the steep, muddy hill.*

clenched: To **clench** is to squeeze together or grab something tightly. *The boy **clenched** his teeth when he was angry. The frightened little girl **clenched** her father's hand.*

compounded: Things that are **compounded** are mixed together to make a whole. *In science class we **compounded** baking soda and vinegar to make a model volcano erupt.* **Compounded** also means added to or increased. *A sudden storm **compounded** the difficulty of sailing the ship.*

concussion: A sudden, violent shaking or shock. *I felt small **concussions** run through my body as my friends and I rode the bumper cars at the carnival.*

confront: To **confront** someone is to face or meet that person directly in a bold or unfriendly way. *I decided to **confront** the bully and tell him to stop being mean to me.*

conjure: To use magic to make something appear or happen. *This magic book will teach you to **conjure** a rabbit out of a top hat.* A **conjure** woman heals or helps people by using magic.

contratista: A Spanish word that means "contractor," a person who agrees to perform work or build something in exchange for money.

Cossacks: People from Russia and Ukraine known for their skill as horseback riders and soldiers.

croaker sack: A bag made of rough cloth used for carrying things.

cynically: When you speak or act **cynically**, you say or do something that shows you expect the worst in a situation. *"Of course it's going to rain at our picnic," she said* **cynically**.

czar: A Russian emperor.

dawdling: When you **dawdle**, you take more time than necessary or do something very slowly. *The teacher told the students* **dawdling** *in the hall to get to class.*

decent: Good, thoughtful, and kind. *It was* **decent** *of my friend to lend me her umbrella during the storm.*

dejected: Sad and gloomy. *The players were* **dejected** *when their team lost the championship game.*

demolishing: To **demolish** something is to knock it down or destroy it. *The wrecking crew is* **demolishing** *the old building.*

deprived: To be **deprived** of something is to have it taken away from you. *My brother was* **deprived** *of his allowance as a punishment for misbehaving.*

despair: Complete loss of hope. *The woman was in* **despair** *after her wallet was stolen.*

detoured: To **detour** is to take a different or longer way to get somewhere, either to avoid something or to stop along the way. *We* **detoured** *through the park on the way home and got back late.*

dignity: A sense of self-respect, pride, and honor. *The baseball team kept their* **dignity** *after losing the game by shaking hands with the winners.*

discarded: To **discard** something is to throw it away. *When the family moved, they **discarded** their old furniture.*

dissolved: To **dissolve** is to disappear or melt into a liquid form. *The sugar **dissolved** quickly into the hot tea.*

drenched: Completely wet. *The man was **drenched** after he fell into the pool.*

droned: To **drone** is to proceed in a boring, dull way. *The weeks before our trip to the amusement park **droned** on until the day finally arrived.*

dutifully: If you do something **dutifully**, you do it because you know you should. *I don't like making my bed, but I do it **dutifully** each morning.*

eavesdropped: To **eavesdrop** is to secretly listen to a conversation. *I got upset when my sister **eavesdropped** on my phone call.*

elaborately: Something done **elaborately** is done with great care or attention to detail. *The girl's **elaborately** braided and curled hairstyle took hours to create.*

emblazoned: Something **emblazoned** is decorated or marked in a bright or attention-getting way. *The knight carried a shield **emblazoned** with a golden dragon.*

enforced: To **enforce** is to make sure a law or rule is followed. *The safety guards **enforced** the rules for crossing the street.*

enthralled: To be **enthralled** means that you are so delighted or amazed by something that you give it your full attention. *The daring circus performers **enthralled** the audience.*

entranced: If you are **entranced**, you are so amazed by something that you forget to pay attention to what's around you. *My sister was so **entranced** by the movie that she didn't hear the doorbell ring.*

era: A period of time marked by important events. *Living in France for ten years was a memorable **era** in my father's life.*

essential: Something **essential** is very important and truly needed. *If you want to go on the field trip, it is **essential** that you bring a permission slip.*

exaggerated: To **exaggerate** is to make something seem bigger, better, or more important than it really is. *We knew his story about catching one hundred fish was **exaggerated** because he has only gone fishing once.*

exception: A person or thing that is different, left out, or doesn't follow the usual rule. *Everyone in my family has brown eyes, but my little brother is the **exception** because he has blue eyes.*

exuberant: High-spirited or full of joy. *The **exuberant** girl hugged her friend, yelling, "I got the lead part in the play!"*

fascinated: To **fascinate** is to capture and hold someone's attention. *The boy was so **fascinated** by the ant farm that he studied it for hours.*

fixedly: If you do something **fixedly**, you do it steadily and firmly. *The cat stared **fixedly** at the birds for almost an hour.*

flourish: A **flourish** is a dramatic movement. *A magician might add a **flourish** when he does a magic trick, like waving his arms or wiggling his fingers.*

flybane: A poisonous mushroom that is red with white spots.

frail: Weak. *After his long illness, the boy was **frail** and got tired easily.*

fringed: Something that is **fringed** has threads or thread-like material all around its edges. *Your eyes are **fringed** with eyelashes. The garden path was **fringed** with tall grasses.*

furrows: Long grooves or ruts. *The farmer had to plow **furrows** in the field before she could plant the corn.*

gave: Moved or broke under force or pressure. *The stuck door **gave** a little when I pushed hard against it.*

ghastly: Something **ghastly** is awful and upsetting. *After the terrible hurricane, the town was a **ghastly** sight.*

gladiolus: A tall flower with many colorful blossoms and long, thin leaves.

gravelly: A **gravelly** sound is low and rough. *Your voice might be **gravelly** after shouting or talking loudly for a long time.*

groats: Kernels of grain that have been crushed or "hulled" (had the outer covering removed).

Groke: A frightening creature that lives in the imaginary land of Moominvalley.

grudging: Something **grudging** is not given in an easy, free way, or is given only because it has been forced. *I could tell she was not really sorry because she gave such a grudging apology.*

haggard: Someone who is **haggard** looks very worried, tired, or worn out. *We could see by her haggard face that she had stayed up far too late.*

harassing: To **harass** is to annoy or bother someone again and again. *The librarian told us to stop harassing her after we'd asked her the same question three times.*

heartily: In a warm, sincere way, or with great energy. *If your friend returned from a long vacation, you might welcome her back heartily.*

homeland: The place or country where you were born and that you think of as your true home. *Although my grandmother has lived in the United States for fifty years, Italy is her homeland.*

horrid: Unpleasant or nasty. *Rotten eggs have a horrid smell. Our horrid neighbors yell at us if we play too close to their house.*

hotfoot it: To leave a place very quickly.

huaraches: Flat-heeled sandals made of woven leather.

hüerquito: A Spanish word that adults often use with children. It means "little one" or "silly one."

humored: When you **humor** someone, you go along with what she wishes so as not to cause trouble. *I didn't want to go to my friend's party, but I humored her and went because I knew she'd be upset otherwise.*

139

Ibo: A group of people from the West African country of Nigeria.

immense: Something **immense** is huge or of great size. *An ocean is an **immense** body of water.*

immobile: Completely still or impossible to move. *The boy was careful to stay **immobile** when the bee landed on his arm. Even though we all pushed it, the heavy car remained **immobile**.*

incredulously: Saying or doing something **incredulously** shows that you do not believe what is happening. *You might stare **incredulously** at an acrobat doing amazing tricks.*

indistinguishable: When people or things are **indistinguishable**, you can't tell the difference between them. *The twins made themselves **indistinguishable** by dressing exactly alike.* Something is also **indistinguishable** when you can't pick it out from its surroundings. *A chameleon can make itself **indistinguishable** from whatever surface it is standing on.*

indolently: When you do something **indolently**, you do it in a lazy way, without trying very hard. *The girl vacuumed the rug so **indolently** that there were still crumbs and dirt all over it when she was done.*

infallible: Certain not to fail. *The bank robbers got away with all the money, thanks to their **infallible** plan.*

insolently: When you do something **insolently**, you do it in a bold or rude manner, without respect. *If you talked back to your teacher, you might be punished for behaving insolently.*

inspection: An **inspection** is a very close and careful look at something. *The handyman did an inspection of our roof to find out where it was leaking.*

institution: A tradition or custom. *Having a big meal on a certain holiday may be an institution in your family.*

intense: To be **intense** is to have or to show strong feeling or great purpose. *The tug-of-war during gym class was very intense because both teams really wanted to win.*

intrigue: Secret or tricky plans, or the process of carrying out those plans. *A spy movie is full of intrigue.*

ironic, ironical: To be **ironic** or **ironical** is to use words to express the opposite of what you really mean or feel. *You are being ironic if you say "Wow, that's great!" when you hear bad news.*

jouncing: When you **jounce**, you bounce or make bumping, jerking movements. *My sister annoyed me by jouncing up and down on my bed.*

kerosene: A thin, colorless liquid fuel that is used to light nonelectric lamps.

kilns: A **kiln** is a very hot oven used to harden, dry, or burn something. *Clay pots need to be dried in kilns before they are finished.*

lapses: A **lapse** is a small failure or mistake. *Her teacher said that her essay was very good, with just a few **lapses** in spelling.*

leech: A kind of worm that survives by attaching itself to an animal and sucking its blood. If you describe someone as a **leech**, you are saying that person takes from others and gives nothing in return. *She is a **leech**, always asking someone else to pay for her when we go out to dinner.*

lunged: To **lunge** is to make a sudden forward movement. *The basketball star **lunged** at the player on the other team and stole the ball.*

luxurious: Something **luxurious** gives you comfort and pleasure. *Lying in the sun on the beach feels very **luxurious**.*

maneuvered: To **maneuver** is to move carefully or skillfully into a certain position. *I **maneuvered** between the wall and the couch to vacuum the small space.*

mannered: If you do or say something in a **mannered** way, you do or say it in a particular way or style. *She eats corn on the cob in a **mannered** way, nibbling one row of kernels at a time.*

marmalade: A jelly made from oranges or other citrus fruit.

matronly: Looking or acting like a married or widowed older woman. *A **matronly** person sometimes behaves in a serious way, like a stern mother.*

melancholy: Sad and gloomy. *You might feel **melancholy** if your best friend moved away.*

menacing: Threatening or dangerous. *The angry man shook his fist in a **menacing** way.*

mincer: A machine that chops food into very small pieces.

misery: A feeling of suffering and great unhappiness. *The flood caused **misery** for many people because it destroyed everything they had.*

negligent: If you are being **negligent**, you aren't paying full attention to what you're doing, or you are acting in a careless way. *She was skimming the pages of her book in a **negligent** way instead of reading closely.*

novelty: Something that is a **novelty** has a new or unusual quality. *My favorite thing about field trips is the **novelty** of leaving school in the middle of the day.*

obsessive: Being **obsessive** about something means you focus on it so much that you have little time to think of other things. *The man's **obsessive** love for cars was the reason he became a mechanic.*

octopi: More than one octopus.

oilskin: Cloth that has been treated with oil to make it waterproof.

overseer: Someone who watches and directs workers.

partitions: A **partition** is a wall or screen that divides a room. *When I shared a room with my sister, we set up **partitions** so we could each have our own space.*

passionately: Something done **passionately** is done with great feeling, excitement, or energy. *If you want* ***passionately*** *to make the basketball team, you might practice every day.*

peanut gallery: A person or group of people whose comments are not considered important. *"It's hard to drive when the* ***peanut gallery*** *in the backseat keeps giving me wrong directions," my mother told us.*

peculiar: Something **peculiar** is strange or unusual, and often has something special about it. *My dog is* ***peculiar*** *because he doesn't like treats.*

piped: To **pipe** is to speak in a high, shrill way. *The small child* ***piped****, "I'm six years old!"*

pitching: Something is **pitching** if it is moving up and down or back and forth with great force. *In an earthquake, the* ***pitching*** *of the ground can cause buildings to crumble and fall.*

plantation farms: Large farms where crops such as coffee, tobacco, or cotton are grown and harvested by workers who live on the property. *Before the Civil War, many slaves were forced to work on* ***plantation farms****.*

porcelain: A type of pottery that is hard and white.

posse: A **posse** is a group of people brought together by a sheriff to help stop crimes. *The sheriff gathered a* ***posse*** *of brave townspeople to help him stop the thieves.* A **posse** is also a small gang or group of people who know each other well. *My older brother and his* ***posse*** *of friends are always playing jokes on me.*

predicament: A **predicament** is a difficult or uncomfortable situation. *You would be in a **predicament** if you locked yourself out of the house and nobody was home.*

predict: To **predict** something is to say that it will happen in the future. *The weathermen **predict** that this summer is going to be one of the hottest ever.*

primly: In a stiff, proper way. *He **primly** touched the corners of his mouth with his napkin after eating his soup.*

progressive: If you are **progressive**, you are in favor of making improvements and changes to old ideas or ways of thinking. *The **progressive** teacher always liked to try new lesson plans and projects with her students.*

pursed: To **purse** your lips is to press them together, usually to show you're annoyed. *The kids knew their mother meant business when she **pursed** her lips and crossed her arms.*

raucous: Noisy and rough-sounding. *The crow gave a raucous cry and flew away.*

reassuringly: Something done **reassuringly** is done in a way to give someone back their confidence. *My father hugged me **reassuringly** when I felt nervous about jumping off the high dive.*

recollection: The act of remembering. *I haven't been to his house in a while, but to the best of my **recollection** it's across the street from the high school.*

reformation: A **reformation** is a change for the better or an improvement in someone or something. *The criminal's **reformation** into a kind, helpful person was remarkable.*

remedies: A **remedy** is something that relieves pain or discomfort, or cures sickness. *There are lots of cold **remedies**, but my favorites are chicken noodle soup and ginger ale.*

renounced: To **renounce** something means to give it up. *She **renounced** piano and chose to play guitar instead.* **Renounce** can also mean to refuse or reject something. *The man **renounced** his old life and was determined to change his ways.*

repercussions: In this story, **repercussions** are the echoes of a loud, deep sound. *The drum created deafening **repercussions** in the large, empty room.*

resilient: Something or someone **resilient** is able to recover from difficult, rough, or painful actions. *A thick plastic cup is **resilient** because it doesn't break if it falls to the floor.*

respective: Belonging to or connected to a particular person or thing. *My cousins and I lived together over the summer and then returned to our **respective** homes in the fall.*

retrieved: To **retrieve** something is to get it back. *My dog **retrieved** the ball I threw and dropped it at my feet.*

ricocheted: If something **ricochets**, it bounces off something and moves in a different direction. *Hail ricocheted off our roof and scattered all over our yard.*

rubbers: Low waterproof shoes worn over regular shoes.

ruble: The main unit of money in Russia.

savored: To **savor** something is to enjoy it greatly or fully. *I savored every minute of my summer vacation.*

serene: Something **serene** is calm and peaceful. *A baby who is fast asleep looks very serene.*

Shabbos: Another word for *Sabbath*, the day of the week used for rest and worship. *For Jewish people, Shabbos begins at sundown on Friday and ends at sundown on Saturday.*

sharecropper: Someone who lives and farms on land that is owned by someone else. *A sharecropper gives part of the farm's crops to the owner as rent.*

simpleton: A **simpleton** is a foolish person, or a person who is easy to trick. *She was such a simpleton that she would believe anything you told her.*

simultaneously: At the same time. *Noise filled the room as all the clocks began to chime simultaneously.*

sin vergüenza: A Spanish phrase meaning "troublemaker" or "rascal."

slackening: To **slacken** is to become slower or less strong. *The runner's speed was slackening after he crossed the finish line.*

snickered: To **snicker** is to quietly laugh in a nasty way. *The boy **snickered** rudely when the substitute teacher tried to make a joke.*

snowy egrets: White birds with long bills and legs.

snuff: A type of tobacco.

species: A **species** is a kind, type, or sort of something. *Hip-hop is a very different **species** of music than classical or rock.*

spindly: When something is **spindly**, it is long, thin, and often weak. *The old chair's **spindly** legs broke when I sat down on it.*

spluttered: When something **splutters**, it makes a repeated noise that sounds like choking or spitting. *The broken car engine **spluttered** loudly and then went completely dead.*

squall: To **squall** is to cry loudly. *The cranky baby began to **squall** at the top of his lungs.*

stammered: When you **stammer**, you speak in an unsure way, stopping often and repeating sounds or words without meaning to. *The nervous girl **stammered** whenever she had to speak in front of the class.*

supple: Something **supple** bends and moves easily. *Dancers need to have **supple** bodies in order to stretch and leap into the air.*

surged: To **surge** is to rush forward like a wave. *When the bell rang for recess, the class **surged** onto the playground.*

surveillance: To do **surveillance** is to watch someone or something very closely. *A private detective does* ***surveillance*** *by following a person and taking pictures of him.*

suspended: Something **suspended** is held or hung up so that it seems like it's floating. *The thin wires holding up the circus performer made it look like she was* ***suspended*** *in the air.*

swaggering: To **swagger** is to walk in a bold, proud, and bragging way. *I could tell that her team had won the game by the way she came* ***swaggering*** *across the field.*

synagogue: A building that is used for Jewish religious services.

systematically: If you do something **systematically**, you do it according to a plan. *My parents do the dishes* ***systematically***—*my father washes them and my mother dries them.*

taquitos: A Mexican dish in which corn or flour tortillas are wrapped around a filling and fried.

tentatively: To do something **tentatively** is to do it in an unsure way. *If you think you know the answer to a question but you aren't sure, you might raise your hand* ***tentatively***.

till: To **till** is to prepare land for planting and raising crops. *A farmer will* ***till*** *the soil by plowing it and making rows to plant seeds.*

timidly: If you do something **timidly**, you do it in a shy and easily frightened way. *My baby sister hides behind me **timidly** when she meets strangers.*

toilet water: Toilet water is a lightly scented perfume that is sprayed on the skin. *I gave my grandmother a bottle of **toilet water** scented like roses for her birthday.*

Torah: In the Jewish religion, the **Torah** is the first five books of the Hebrew Bible.

transformed: When you **transform** something, you change it into something else or make it look very different. *The artist **transformed** the lump of clay into a vase. A crib and some stuffed animals **transformed** the spare bedroom into a nursery.*

tremendously: Greatly or extremely. *You might be **tremendously** happy to meet someone famous, like your favorite movie star or athlete.*

tremor: A shaking or vibrating movement. *The **tremor** in the old man's hand caused the teacup he was holding to rattle.*

truce: An agreement to stop fighting, at least for a short time. *After arguing for an hour, the two men finally reached a **truce** and shook hands.*

tumultuously: In a disorderly, energetic way. *A flock of pigeons landed **tumultuously** to peck at the scattered breadcrumbs.*

unsettling: Upsetting or disturbing. *My parents think that the horror movie will be too **unsettling** for my little brother to watch.*

valise: A small suitcase.

vandals: A **vandal** is a person who destroys public or private property on purpose. ***Vandals** had spray-painted the wall of the building during the night.*

veranda: A porch that wraps around the outside of a house.

vital: When something is **vital**, it is necessary or very important. *Air, water, and food are **vital** for your body to function.*

warily: Cautiously. *She checked **warily** over her shoulder to see if anyone was following her.*

welding: To **weld** is to join different pieces of metal by heating them and then pressing or hammering them together. *The statue was made by **welding** pieces of bronze together.*

wide berth: To give something a wide berth is to stay a good distance away from it, often to avoid harm. *We gave my dad and uncle a **wide berth** so that they could bring the new sofa into the house.*

wielding: To **wield** is to hold or handle something with skill. *The knight charged into battle **wielding** a sword.*

ACKNOWLEDGMENTS

All possible care has been taken to trace ownership and secure permission for each selection in this series. The Great Books Foundation wishes to thank the following authors, publishers, and representatives for permission to reproduce copyrighted material:

Charles, from THE LOTTERY, by Shirley Jackson. Copyright © 1948, 1949 by Shirley Jackson. Copyright renewed 1976, 1977 by Laurence Hyman, Barry Hyman, Mrs. Sarah Webster, and Mrs. Joanne Schnurer. Reproduced by permission of Farrar, Straus and Giroux, LLC.

The Special Powers of Blossom Culp, by Richard Peck, from BIRTHDAY SURPRISES, edited by Johanna Hurwitz, published by HarperCollins Children's Books. Copyright © 1995 by Richard Peck. Reproduced by permission of Sheldon Fogleman Agency on behalf of the author.

THE PEDDLER'S GIFT, by Maxine Rose Schur. Copyright © 1999 by Maxine Rose Schur. Reproduced by permission of Dial Books for Young Readers, a division of Penguin Group (USA) Inc.

IN THE TIME OF THE DRUMS, by Kim L. Siegelson. Copyright © 1999 by Kim L. Siegelson. Reproduced by permission of Disney-Hyperion, an imprint of Disney Book Group LLC.

Learning the Game, from THE CIRCUIT: STORIES FROM THE LIFE OF A MIGRANT CHILD, by Francisco Jiménez. Copyright © 1997 by Francisco Jiménez. Reproduced by permission of the University of New Mexico Press.

The Invisible Child, from TALES FROM MOOMIN VALLEY, by Tove Jansson. Copyright © 1962 by Tove Jansson. Reproduced by permission of Farrar, Straus, and Giroux, LLC.

THE COMING OF THE SURFMAN, by Peter Collington. Copyright © 1993 by Peter Collington. Reproduced by permission of David Higham Associates, agent for the author.

All Summer in a Day, from THE STORIES OF RAY BRADBURY, by Ray Bradbury. Copyright © 1954, renewed 1982 by Ray Bradbury. Originally appeared in *Magazine of Fantasy and Science Fiction*. Reproduced by permission of Don Congdon Associates, Inc.

A GAME OF CATCH, by Richard Wilbur. Copyright © 1953 by Richard Wilbur. First published in the *New Yorker*, July 15, 1953. Reproduced by permission of Harcourt Children's Books, an imprint of Houghton Mifflin Harcourt Publishing Company.